A

MANUAL OF CONCHOLOGY,

ACCORDING

TO THE SYSTEM LAID DOWN

BY LAMARCK,

WITH THE LATE IMPROVEMENTS

BY DE BLAINVILLE.

EXEMPLIFIED AND ARRANGED FOR THE USE OF STUDENTS.

BY THOMAS WYATT, M.A.

ILLUSTRATED BY THIRTY-SIX PLATES CONTAINING MORE THAN TWO HUNDRED
TYPES, DRAWN FROM THE NATURAL SHELL.

NEW-YORK:
HARPER & BROTHERS, CLIFF-STREET.
1838.

Entered, according to Act of Congress, in the year 1838, by
THOMAS WYATT,
in the Clerk's Office of the Eastern District of Pennsylvania.

INTRODUCTION.

Conchology or Testaceolgy is a numerous and beautiful branch of Natural History, treating of the testaceous covering of animals; perhaps none but the department of Flora can vie with it in variety, symmetry of form, and rich colouring. It has ever excited admiration, and obtained a prominent situation in the cabinet; and so great are the facilities afforded at the present day to procure specimens and obtain a knowledge of this science, that it has become one of the requisites of a finished education. Shells are found in all parts of the world, both on land and in water; but the most beautiful and valuable species are found between the tropics.

At first they were regarded as pleasing curiosities, and prized only on that account; but the investigations of scientific men have proved that the study of this science is not only interesting, but useful. Much valuable information has already been obtained, and, from the investigations of modern naturalists, much more may be anticipated.

So intimate is the connexion between Conchology and Geology, that a knowledge of the one is indispensable to the study and acquirement of the other. The geologist will draw much advantage from a close study of the testaceous covering of molluscous animals to aid him in determining the identity or the superposition of the different strata of the earth and the extraordinary changes it has undergone; for, as Bergman elegantly says, "fossil shells, coral, and wood are the only three remaining medals of Creation." He will see in the innumerable quantity of these animals, succeeding each other from generation to generation in the depth of the seas, one of the evident causes of the growth and increase of islands and continents.

But man may find in the knowledge of Mollusca applications still more direct to his well being in society, both as to the advantages and disadvantages to be derived from them: thus a great number of species are proper for food, as oysters, muscles, &c., which are objects of commercial speculations. The Pinna furnishes the Italians with materials for a rich dress, and the pearl, so much prized by the Orientals, by princes, and particularly by the ladies, as a modest and beautiful ornament, is produced by a disease of the animals in certain species of shells. It was this knowledge which made the celebrated Linnæus imagine that it was possible to form an artificial pearlery in the rivers of Sweden. The mother of pearl, so much employed as an ornament in articles of luxury, is only the interior lining of certain univalve or bivalve shells. Painting draws from some of these animals many colours, valuable not so much for their beauty as their usefulness, as Chinese ink and sepia.

The brightest and richest colour known by the ancients, and used by them for the celebrated Tyrian purple die, is produced by animals at this time known by the name of Purpura.

The Teredo attacks the wood of our vessels, and often does much injury; therefore the knowledge of its manners,

INTRODUCTION.

habits, and customs must be of great importance in countries infested with them, so as to be able to provide a remedy against them. Snails and slugs are also enemies much to be dreaded in our gardens.

Lamarck, in his last work, the result of the successive and continual labours of his whole life and those of his contemporaries, has rendered a very great service to science, but especially to conchology, by describing, or, at least, characterizing the numerous species of shells in his own splendid cabinet. It may be proper here to remark, that a part of Lamarck's cabinet is now in the possession of Isaac Lea, Esq., of Philadelphia, to whom we are much indebted for valuable assistance. To Dr. Comstock, and the Rev. W. Turner, of Hartford, Conn., we are much indebted for kind favours; their aid has greatly facilitated our labours.

In this Manual of Conchology we have endeavoured to give a free translation of Lamarck's system, as simplified by De Blainville; and, in order to facilitate as much as possible the study of this beautiful and interesting science, we have divested it of numerous technicalities, and divided it into four classes: Annelides, Cirrhipedes, Conchifera, and Mollusca.

To each class we have assigned its various families, to each family its genera, and to each genus its living species; thereby making it plain and within the reach of the meanest capacity. A type of almost every genus is given, excepting only those shells which, from their similarity to other genera, may easily be classed.

It was deemed advisable, as this is intended for an easy introduction to the science, to omit many divisions and subdivisions, which would only serve to perplex and render the attainment more difficult.

As the Naiades, or shells of this country, are given in several valuable scientific works lately published, we have only slightly touched them in the place they are intended to occupy.

We cannot expect that the work now presented to the public is free from imperfections; but we ask for their lenity and kind forbearance to excuse whatever defects there may be in our humble attempts to advance the cause of science. Conchology, like other departments of natural history, is progressing; and that which is given to-day is almost always susceptible of being modified to-morrow; should this work be well received, it is our intention to give, as soon as practicable, an enlarged work, containing even the minute microscopic shells and the fossils, with plates containing types of as many species of the genera as can possibly be obtained.

The plates were drawn and coloured with great care and accuracy from the natural shells in our own cabinet, under the superintendence of Mr. James Ackerman, artist.

T. W,

ARRANGEMENT.

CLASS I.
ANNELIDES.
FOUR FAMILIES.

Fam.
1. *Dorsaliæ.* Two genera.
   1. Arenicola. Species 1
   2. Siliquaria. " 4
2. *Maldaniæ.* Two genera.
   1. Clymene. Species 1
   2. Dentalium. " 12
3. *Amphitritæa.* Four genera.
   1. Pectinaria. Species 2
   2. Sabellaria. " 2
   3. Terebella. " 3
   4. Amphitrite. " 6
4. *Serpulacea.* Five genera.
   1. Spirorbis. Species 5
   2. Serpula. " 26
   3. Vermilia. " 8
   4. Galeolaria. " 2
   5. Magilus. " 1

CLASS II.
CIRRHIPEDES.
ONE FAMILY.

1. *Cirrhipedes.* Ten genera.
   1. Tubicinella. Species 1
   2. Coronula. " 3
   3. Balanus. " 28
   4. Acasta. " 3
   5. Creusia. " 3
   6. Pyrgoma. " 1
   7. Anatifera. " 5
   8. Pollicipes. " 3
   9. Cineras. " 1
   10. Otion. " 2

CLASS III.
CONCHIFERA.
TWENTY FAMILIES.

1. *Tubicola.* Six genera.
   1. Aspergillum. Species 4

Fam.
   2. Clavagella. Species 1
   3. Fistulana. " 4
   4. Septaria. " 1
   5. Teredina. " 2
   6. Teredo. " 2
2. *Pholadaria.* Two genera.
   1. Pholas. Species 9
   2. Gastrochæna. " 3
3. *Solenides.* Four genera.
   1. Solen. Species 18
   2. Panopæa. " 1
   3. Solecurtus. " 3
   4. Glycimeris. " 1
4. *Myaria.* Two genera.
   1. Mya. Species 4
   2. Anatina. " 10
5. *Mactracea.* Seven genera.
   1. Lutraria. Species 11
   2. Mactra. " 33
   3. Crassatella. " 11
   4. Erycina. " 1
   5. Ungulina. " 2
   6. Solenimya. " 2
   7. Amphidesma. " 16
6. *Corbulacea.* Two genera.
   1. Corbula. Species 9
   2. Pandora. " 2
7. *Lithophagi.* Three genera.
   1. Saxicava. Species 5
   2. Petricola. " 13
   3. Venerirupis. " 7
8. *Nymphacea.* Ten genera.
   1. Sanguinolaria. Species 4
   2. Psammobia. " 18
   3. Psammotæa. " 7
   4. Tellina. " 54
   5. Tellinides. " 1
   6. Corbis. " 1
   7. Lucina. " 20
   8. Donax. " 27
   9. Capsa. " 2
   10. Crassina. " 1
9. *Conchacea.* Seven genera.
   1. Cyclas. Species 11
   2. Cyrena. " 10

Fam.			Fam.		
3. Galathea.	Species	1	3. Vulsella.	Species	6
4. Cyprina.	"	2	4. Placuna.	"	3
5. Cytherea.	"	78	5. Anomia.	"	9
6. Venus.	"	88	6. Crania.	"	1
7. Venericardia.	"	1	20. *Brachiopoda.* Three genera.		

10. *Cardiacea.* Five genera.
    1. Cardium.   Species 48
    2. Cardita.   " 21
    3. Cypricardia. " 4
    4. Hiatella.   " 2
    5. Isocardia. " 3

11. *Arcacea.* Four genera.
    1. Cucullæa.   Species 1
    2. Arca.   " 37
    3. Pectunculus. " 19
    4. Nucula.   " 6

12. *Trigonacea.* Two genera.
    1. Trigonia.   Species 1
    2. Castalia.   " 1

13. *Naiades.* Four genera.
    1. Unio.   Species 48
    2. Hyria.   " 2
    3. Anodonta.   " 15
    4. Iridina.   " 1

14. *Chamacea.* Three genera.
    1. Diceras.   Species 1
    2. Chama.   " 17
    3. Etheria.   " 4

15. *Tridacnites.* Two genera.
    1. Tridacna.   Species 6
    2. Hippopus.   " 1

16. *Mytilacea.* Three genera.
    1. Mytilus.   Species 35
    2. Modiola.   " 23
    3. Pinna.   " 15

17. *Malleacea.* Five genera.
    1. Crenatula. Species 7
    2. Perna.   " 10
    3. Malleus.   " 6
    4. Avicula.   " 13
    5. Meleagrina. " 2

18. *Pectinides.* Seven genera.
    1. Pedum.   Species 1
    2. Lima.   " 6
    3. Pecten.   " 59
    4. Plagiostoma. " 10
    5. Plicatula. " 5
    6. Spondylus. " 21
    7. Podopsis.   " 2

19. *Ostracea.* Six genera.
    1. Gryphæa.   Species 1
    2. Ostrea.   " 48

   1. Orbicula.   Species 1
   2. Terebratula. " 12
   3. Lingula.   " 1

CLASS IV.
MOLLUSCA.

TWENTY-TWO FAMILIES.

1. *Pteropoda.* Six genera.
    1. Hyalæa.   Species 2
    2. Clio.   " 2
    3. Cleodora. " 2
    4. Limacina. " 1
    5. Cymbulia. " 1
    6. Pneumodermon. " 1

2. *Phyllidiacea.* Four genera.
    1. Phyllidia. Species 3
    2. Chitonellus. " 2
    3. Chiton.   " 6
    4. Patella.   " 45

3. *Calyptracea.* Seven genera.
    1. Parmophora. Species 3
    2. Emarginula. " 4
    3. Fissurella. " 19
    4. Pileopsis. " 4
    5. Calyptræa. " 4
    6. Crepidula. " 6
    7. Ancylus.   " 2

4. *Bullacea.* Three genera.
    1. Acera.   Species 1
    2. Bullæa.   " 1
    3. Bulla.   " 11

5. *Aplysiacea.* Two genera.
    1. Aplysia.   Species 3
    2. Dolabella. " 2

6. *Limacinea.* Five genera.
    1. Onchidium. Species 2
    2. Parmacella. " 1
    3. Limax.   " 4
    4. Testacella. " 1
    5. Vitrina.   " 1

7. *Colimacea.* Eleven genera.
    1. Helix.   Species 107
    2. Carocolla. " 15
    3. Anostoma. " 2
    4. Helicina. " 4
    5. Pupa.   " 27

ARRANGEMENT.

Fam.		
6. Clausilia.	Species	12
7. Bulimus.	"	34
8. Achatina.	"	20
9. Succinea.	"	3
10. Auricula.	"	14
11. Cyclostoma.	"	28

8. *Lymnæcea.* Three genera.
1. Planorbis.	Species	12
2. Physa.	"	4
3. Lymnæa.	"	11

9. *Melanides.* Three genera.
1. Melania.	Species	16
2. Melanopsis.	"	3
3. Pyrena.	"	4

10. *Peristomides.* Three gen.
1. Valvata.	Species	1
2. Paludina.	"	7
3. Ampullaria.	"	11

11. *Neritacea.* Five genera.
1. Neritina.	Species	21
2. Navicella.	"	3
3. Nerita.	"	17
4. Natica.	"	31
5. Janthina.	"	2

12. *Macrostomides.* Four gen.
1. Sigaretus.	Species	4
2. Stomatella.	"	5
3. Stomatia.	"	2
4. Haliotis.	"	15

13. *Plicacea.* Two genera.
1. Tornatella.	Species	6
2. Pyramidella.	"	5

14. *Scalarides.* Three genera.
1. Vermetus.	Species	1
2. Scalaria.	"	7
3. Delphinula.	"	3

15. *Turbinacea.* Seven genera.
1. Solarium.	Species	7
2. Trochus.	"	69
3. Monodonta.	"	23
4. Turbo.	"	34
5. Planaxis.	"	2
6. Phasianella.	"	10
7. Turritella.	"	13

16. *Canalifera.* Eleven genera.
1. Cerithium.	Species	36
2. Pleurotoma.	Species	23
3. Turbinella.	"	23
4. Cancellaria.	"	12
5. Fasciolaria.	"	8
6. Fusus.	"	37
7. Pyrula.	"	28
8. Struthiolaria.	"	2
9. Ranella.	"	14
10. Murex.	"	86
11. Triton.	"	31

17. *Alata.* Three genera.
1. Rostellaria.	Species	3
2. Pteroceras.	"	7
3. Strombus.	"	32

18. *Purpurifera.* Eleven gen.
1. Cassidaria.	Species	5
2. Cassis.	"	25
3. Ricinula.	"	9
4. Purpura.	"	50
5. Monoceros.	"	5
6. Concholepas.	"	1
7. Harpa.	"	8
8. Dolium.	"	7
9. Buccinum.	"	58
10. Eburna.	"	5
11. Terebra.	"	24

19. *Columellaria.* Five genera.
1. Columbella.	Species	18
2. Mitra,	"	80
3. Voluta.	"	44
4. Marginella.	"	24
5. Volvaria.	"	5

20. *Convoluta.* Six genera.
1. Ovula.	Species	12
2. Cypræa.	"	68
3. Terebellum.	"	1
4. Ancillaria.	"	4
5. Oliva.	"	62
6. Conus.	"	181

21. *Nautilacea.* Two genera.
1. Spirula.	Species	1
2. Nautilus.	"	2

22. *Heteropoda.* Two genera.
1. Argonauta.	Species	3
2. Carinaria.	"	3

CONCHOLOGY.

CLASS I.

ANNELIDES.
CONTAINS FOUR FAMILIES.

FAMILY I.
DORSALIÆ. Two genera.

1. Arenicola. Has no shell. One species.
A. piscatorium.

2. Siliquaria. Four species.

Shell very thin, conical, tubular, involuted in a loose and irregular spiral manner; aperture circular, edges sharp, interrupted in the middle by a notch prolonged like a slit through nearly all its length, stopped abruptly at some distance from the summit.

Siliquaria anguina.   Siliquaria lævigatæ.
S. muricata.   S. lactea.

S. anguina. The Snake Siliquaria. Pl. 33, fig. 4.
Shell tapering, undulating, spiral at the extremity.

S. muricata. The Prickly Siliquaria.
Species armed with short spines or prickles; aperture sometimes margined; usually of a rosy or pink colour.

FAMILY II.

MALDANIÆ. Two genera.

1. Clymene. One species.

C. amphistoma. The double-mouthed Clymene.

Tube thin and slender, open at both ends; incrusted externally with sand and fragments of shells.

2. Dentalium. The Tooth Shell. Twelve species.

This genus took its name from its resemblance to an elephant's tooth. It is an attenuated conical tube, slightly bent, and open at both ends.

Shell tubular, regular, symmetrical, lightly curved longitudinally, conic, attenuated insensibly posteriorly, and open at each extremity by a round orifice.

Dentalium elephantinum.	Dentalium octoganum.
D. aprinum.	D. novemcostatum.
D. fasciatum.	D. dentale.
D. entale.	D. nigrum.
D. Tarentinum.	D. politum.
D. corneum.	D. eburneum.

D. elephantinum. The Elephant's Tooth Shell.

Species in which the tube is striated or ribbed longitudinally; the ribs are generally ten in number; green colour.

D. entale. The common Dentalium. Pl. 33, fig. 1.

Species very minutely striated; white or yellowish colour.

D. pellucidum. The pellucid Dentalium.

Species narrow and thin; pale topaz colour.

D. politum. The ring-striated Tooth Shell.

Species finely pointed, solid, striated annularly; generally rosy or pink colour.

D. rectum. The straight Tooth Shell.

Species entirely straight, with longitudinal ribs.

D. eburneum. The Ivory Tooth Shell.

Species of a reddish or pale yellow colour, with the tip frequently tinged with orange or pink.

FAMILY III.

AMPHITRITÆA. Four genera.

The similarity of the four genera comprising this family is such, that it was thought sufficient to give only one type (the sabellaria crassissima), as the student may easily recognise the others.

1. Pectinaria. Two species.

A membranous or papyraceous tube, in the form of a reversed cone; unfixed; exterior covered with sandy adhesions.

Pectinaria Belgica. Pectinaria capensis.

P. Belgica. The Belgic Pectinaria.

Tube inversely conic, membranous, and covered with sand.

2. Sabellaria. Two species.

The covering of the animal belonging to this genus is composed of fragments and particles of marine substances, adhering to a tubular membrane; some are detached and others are fixed. The tubes are cellular at the base, and the orifice expanded.

Sabellaria alveolata. Sabellaria crassissima.

S. alveolata. The Honeycomb Sabellaria.

Consists of numerous parallel tubes, nearly straight, communicating by an aperture, forming when in mass the appearance of a honeycomb; it adheres to rocks in clusters.

S. crassissima. The very thick or strong Sabellaria. Pl. 33, fig. 2.

Species incrusted with small stones; sometimes found thick and of a large size.

3. Terebella. Three species.

Tube elongated, cylindrical, membranous, attenuated and pointed at the base, with adhesions of sand.

Terebella conchilega. Terebella cristata.
T. ventricosa.

T. conchilega. The shelly Terebella.
Tube covered with numerous fragments of broken shells.

4. Amphitrite. Six species.

Nearly the same as the Terebella, but of a tougher membranous texture, and generally without adhesions.

Amphitrite ventilabrum. Amphitrite vesiculosa.
A. penicillus. A. volutacornis.
A. magnifica. A. infundibulum.

A. ventilabrum. The Fan Amphitrite.
Tube subulate, smooth, of a yellowish colour.

FAMILY IV.

SERPULACEA. Five genera.

1. Spirorbis. Five species.

Tube testaceous, spirally twisted on a horizontal plane, with terminal aperture rounded or angular, attached by the lower part to marine substances.

Spirorbis Nautiloides. Spirorbis carinata.
S. spirillum. S. lamellosa.
S. tricostalis.

S. Nautiloides. The Nautilus-shaped Spirorbis.
White, transversely wrinkled and minute.

2. Serpula. The Worm Shell. Twenty-six species.

The name of this genus is derived from the Latin word serpo, to creep, on account of the vermiform character of some of its species.

They are invariably tubular, sometimes solitary, but more

frequently in clusters spirally entwined, adhering to marine substances. In colour they are brown, purple, yellow, tawny, pink or white, and sometimes tinged with green.

Tube solid, calcareous, irregularly twisted, fixed to other substances.

Serpula vermicularis.	Serpula filaria.
S. fascicularis.	S. pellucida.
S. intestinum.	S. intorta.
S. contortuplicata.	S. cristata.
S. plicaria.	S. spirulæa.
S. glomerata.	S. quadrangularis.
S. decussata.	S. minima.
S. protensa.	S. echinata.
S. infundibulum.	S. sulcata.
S. annulata.	S. costalis.
S. cereolus.	S. dentifera.
S. filograna.	S. sipho.
S. vermicella.	S. arenaria.

S. vermicularis. The worm-like Serpula.

White, cylindrical, tapering, rugged, variously curved and twisted.

3. Vermilia.   Eight species.

Tube testaceous, cylindrical, more or less twisted, gradually attenuated posteriorly; opening round, the margin with one, two, or three teeth; shell adhering by the side to other substances; provided with a convex operculum.

Vermilia rostrata.	Vermilia subcrenata.
V. triquetra.	V. plicifera.
V. bicarinata.	V. scabra.
V. eruca.	V. tæniata.

V. triquetra. The three-sided Vermilia.

White or reddish, rugged, twisted and triangular, carinated along the back.

4. Galeolaria. Two species.

Distinguished from the Vermilia by a very peculiar operculum. Found in groups, adhering together at the base.

Tube open at the summit; aperture orbicular, terminated on the side by a spatulous tongue; operculum orbicular, squamose, consisting of from five to nine testaceous parts or valves, all attached to one side of the operculum; the middle one dentated at the truncated part of its summit, the others a little toothed on their internal edge.

Galeolaria cæspitosa.   Galeolaria elongata.

G. elongata. The elongated Galeolaria.

Whitish, existing in congregated masses; operculum as above.

5. Magilus. One species.

A very singular shell, greatly resembling a petrified body, composed of a testaceous white substance like alabaster. The base is bent into a short spire, with about four contiguous whorls; the last prolonged and nearly straight. The animal, as it increases in size, abandons the spiral part by increasing the tubular part, filling up the part it quits with calcareous matter, which proves that it advances gradually.

Tube partially involuted, convex in its upper exterior part, the lower side flattened, platted, carinated, and somewhat angular; the spire short, helix-formed, and prolonged through the rest of its extent in nearly a right line; aperture entire, oval, with a sort of sinus or gutter in the middle line, producing the keel of the shell.

M. antiquus. The antiquated Magilus.

Answers to the above description; colour pale yellowish brown, transversely wrinkled.

CLASS II.

CIRRHIPEDES.
HAS BUT ONE FAMILY.

CIRRHIPEDES. Ten genera.

Lamarck divided the Lepas of Linnæus into the various genera which compose this family. The term lepas is derived from the Greek word λεπας, a rock, alluding to its custom of adhering to rocks and marine bodies. The shell often varies in shape, covering, and colouring; it is generally conical, but sometimes hemispherical; some of the valves are placed perpendicularly on a base, broad at the lower margin and tapering towards the summit, which is closed by small horizontal valves forming the operculum. The number of valves is indefinite, from four to twenty-four; but all are diversified with striæ, ridges, and grooves. The striæ are mostly transverse, and the ridges longitudinal.

The valves which compose the operculum or lid vary in shape, and are in number two, three, four, or more; they are generally attached to a ligament.

They are seldom, if ever, found detached, but adhere in groups to rocks, shells, anchors, marine animals, &c. Those that fix themselves to ships are generally called barnacles; they rapidly increase in size and number, do great damage, and greatly impede the progress of the vessel. Some of this family are affixed at the base of the shell to other substances, and are therefore called sessile; others are attached to a fleshy peduncle or stem, and are said to be pedunculated. The peduncle or stem, proceeding from the base of the shell to the substance which sustains it, is sometimes smooth, fine in texture, and tinged with bright red or orange; sometimes it is of a dark or brownish colour, with a texture much coarser and granulated.

1. Tubicinella. One species.

Has the form of a cylindrical tube, slightly curved, and open at both ends; one extremity closed by four trapezoidal valves attached to the inner margin, the other end closed by a membrane. The annular ribs which separate the compartments show its progressive growth. Found buried so deeply in the fat of marine animals, particularly whales, that only the operculum and the upper part of the tube are visible. Shell rather elevated, sub-cylindrical, the partitions rather small and indented; the spaces or compartments almost quadrilateral; the inferior much more narrow than the others; the apertures equal and circular; the membrane which closes the superior forming a tube between the four almost equal valves of the operculum.

T. balænarum. The Whale Tubicinella.

Tubular, with transverse ribs, and a ring-shaped margin; operculum bottle-shaped.

2. Coronula. Three species.

Found imbedded in the skin of whales and other marine animals, though not generally at so great a depth as the Tubicinella. Shell in form a little variable and without trace of support; the coronary part formed of six pieces, as in those properly called *Balanus*, but more regularly disposed in a manner to imitate a kind of crown or tube; spaces alternately hollowed and saliant; operculum not articulated, composed of two pairs of small, level, delicate valves, joined at the aperture of the tube by a considerable membranous part, leaving a passage for the cirrhous appendages of the animal.

Coronula testudinaria.	Coronula diadema.
C. balænarum.	C. quinquevalvis.

C. testudinaria. The Tortoise Coronula.

Very depressed, circular, as if radiated by the disposition of marked spaces, striated transversely, forming six rays diverging from the centre to the circumference; aperture oval and hexagonal.

C. balænarum. The Whale Coronula.

A little more elevated; the spaces prominent, equal between them, much larger than the excavated; the aperture subcircular; the operculum of four valves, almost equal, occupying but a small space of the membranous part which forms between them a sort of tube.

C. diadema. The Crown Coronula.

More elevated, sub-hexagonal; the spaces almost equal, the hollow parts larger than the saliant; the superior aperture very large and hexagonal; the inferior much smaller, of the same form, and communicating in a round excavation by radiated plates; the operculum bivalve.

C. quinquevalvis. The five-valved Coronula. Pl. 4, fig. 3.

Species irregular, having only five valves, of a purple hue.

3. Balanus. The Acorn Shell. Twenty-eight species.

So named from its resemblance to an acorn. Shell conical; the coronary part formed of six very distinct valves, one dorsal, one ventral, and two pairs of laterals, with or without a calcareous support; operculum of four articulated pieces, forming a sort of pyramid in the superior aperture of the tube.

Balanus angulosus.
B. sulcatus.
B. tintinnabulum.
B. nigrescens.
B. cylindraceus.
B. calycularis.
B. roseus.

Balanus palmatus.
B. stalactiferus.
B. plicatus.
B. duploconus.
B. patellaris.
B. semiplicatus.
B. galeatus.

B. ovularis.	B. subimbricatus.
B. miser.	B. rugosus.
B. amphimorphus.	B. placianus.
B. perforatus.	B. crispatus.
B. lævis.	B. punctatus.
B. spinosus.	B. fistulosus.
B. radiatus.	B. latus.

B. sulcatus. The furrowed Balanus.

White; valves nearly smooth; operculum strongly ridged transversely, with longitudinal, nearly obsolete striæ.

B. tintinnabulum. The little Bell Balanus. Pl. 4, fig. 1.

Shell conical; valves strongly and irregularly ribbed; interstices delicately striated transversely; colour purple.

B. spinosus. The spiny Balanus.

Either has no support or a membranous one; armed with spines exteriorly.

4. Acasta. Three species.

Found in sponge, from which, when detached, it cannot stand erect on account of the convexity of the base.

Shell oval, subconic, shaped like a Patella, with six lateral unequal valves slightly connected; operculum with four valves.

Acasta Montagui.   Acasta glans.
A. sulcata.

A. Montagui. Montague's Acasta.

Valves erect, triangular, acute, with muricated ascending spines.

5. Creusia. Three species.

The shells of this genus are generally small; found in the seas of hot countries attached to madrepore and other marine substances.

Shell sessile, thin, Patella-shaped; aperture oval, rather large, closed by a large sub-pyramidal bivalve operculum; a considerable calcareous support, funnel-shaped, penetrating the bodies to which the animal is attached.

 Creusia stromia.   Creusia spinulosa.
     C. verruca.

C. spinulosa. The spiny Creusia.

Very depressed, striated, sometimes with marks of division into four pieces; operculum bivalve.

C. verruca. The warted Creusia. Pl. 4, fig. 2.

Whitish, slightly depressed, with interwoven obliquely striated valves; the margin at the base irregularly serrated.

    6. Pyrgoma. One species.

The principal difference between this genus and the Creusia is in form.

Shell sessile, rather globular appearance on account of the valves being more closely united, ventricose, convex above, apex perforated, aperture small and elliptical; operculum bivalve.

P. cancellata. The cancellated Pyrgoma.

Thick, conical, Patella-shaped, ribs radiating from the summit to the base; aperture very small, closed by an operculum of which the two pieces are long and narrow on each side; pale violet colour.

    7. Anatifera. Five species.

The shells of this genus and the three following genera are affixed to marine bodies by a tough membranous peduncle, varying in length.

Shell flat, with five valves imbricating more or less on the edges, united by a thin membrane.

 Anatifera lævis.   **Anatifera dentata.**
 A. villosa.   A. striata.
     A. vitrea.

A. lævis. The smooth Anatifera. Pl. 4, fig. 5.

Five smooth valves; the dorsal one rounded at the sides,

and slightly carinated; peduncle long, naked, of a scarlet colour.

8. Pollicipes. Three species.

Easily distinguished by the numerous small valves situated at the base.

Pollicipes cornucopia.   Pollicipes mitella.
P. scalpellum.

P. cornucopia. The Cornucopia Pollicipes. Pl. 4, fig. 6.
Peduncle covered with imbricated scales, the lower ones rounded and turned upward.

P. mitella. The Mitre Pollicipes. Pl. 4, fig. 4.
Valves indefinite in number, from six to twenty-four; almost equal, and open like tulips; colour bluish, purplish, brownish, or reddish cast.

9. Cineras. One species.

Shell composed of five testaceous oblong valves, separate, not covering the whole of the body; two at the sides of the aperture, the others on the back; peduncle of a greenish colour, with six longitudinal stripes.

C. vittata. The filleted Cineras.
Answers to the above description.

10. Otion. Two species.

Shell composed of two testaceous valves, enclosed in a mantle or membranous bag, which is prolonged and terminated in two fleshy tubes formed like ears, one of the two having a lateral opening.

Otion Cuvierii.   Otion Blainvillii.

O. Cuvierii. Cuvier's Otion.
Answers to the above.

O. Blainvilli. Blainville's Otion.
Ash coloured; the body and ears spotted with black.

CLASS III.

CONCHIFERA.
CONTAINS TWENTY FAMILIES,

FAMILY I.
TUBICOLA. Six genera.

1. *Aspergillum.* The Watering-pot Shell. Four species.

A well-known but rare shell; the larger end closed by a convex disk, with numerous small perforations, and encircled by a dilated margin of elegant papyraceous tubes, resembling a beautifully plaited ruff; the smaller end open. Found in sandy places at low water.

Shell oval, slightly elongated, striated longitudinally, sub-equilateral; adhering, more or less confounded with the coats of a rather thick calcareous tube, conic, club-shaped, open at its attenuated extremity, and terminated at the other by a convex disk pierced by a great number of sub-tubular, rounded holes, and by a fissure in the centre.

Aspergillum Javanum.   Aspergillum Novæ Zeylandiæ.
A. vaginiferum.   A. agglutinans.

A. Javanum. The Java Aspergillum. Pl. 33, fig. 3.
Species smooth, in which the circumference of the disk is bordered with a waved testaceous fringe.

A. Novæ Zeylandiæ. The New-Zealand Aspergillum.
Species in which the circumference of the disk is without a fringe.

2. Clavagella. One species.

An irregular tube, with branches or projecting tubes at the closed end; within it is one free or moveable valve, united by a ligament to another, which is blended with the tube; this distinguishes it from the Aspergillum. Found in sand and coral.

Shell oval, very slightly elongated, striated longitudinally, slightly irregular; equivalve, inequilateral; hinge a little variable.; ligament exterior; two well-marked distant muscular impressions; a calcareous sub-cylindrical tube, more or less completely surrounding the shell, and terminated before by a single orifice.

C. aperta. The open Clavagella.

Tube erect, adhering; aperture waved, entire, expanding, funnel-shaped, leaving the two valves open or uncovered in all their anterior part; with an ovate face valve.

3. Fistulana. Four species.

Lamarck asserts that the tube and shell of this genus are quite distinct. It so greatly resembles the Teredo that it is with difficulty distinguished. It is found in sand, wood, stone, and sometimes shells.

Shell annular or very short, not sharp nor angular anteriorly, but in other respects much like that of the Teredo.

Tube generally shorter, thicker, more solid, more club-shaped than that of the Teredo, always closed at its anterior extremity in such a manner as to contain and entirely hide the shell; the posterior extremity open, and divided interiorly into two syphons by a partition.

Fistulana clava. Fistulana gregata.
F. corniformis. F. lagenula.

F. corniformis. The horn-shaped Fistulana.
Answers to the above description.

F. gregata. The gregarious Fistulana.
Sheath or tube doubly club-shaped, congregating; shell angularly arcuated, with double angulated serrated wings.

F. Clava. The Club Fistulana. Pl. 33, fig. 5.
Species with one end clavate, the other incurved, narrow-

er, obtuse, and perforated in the middle; shell generally flexuous, of a brownish colour; exterior rough, interior smooth.

4. Septaria. One species.

The tube of this genus unquestionably contains a bivalve shell; but, as no perfect specimen has yet been found, nothing decisive is known respecting it.

Tube calcareous, thick, conically elongated, more or less flexuous, as if composed of pieces placed on the ends of each other, or as if articulated, with a ring or projection more or less marked at the place of the joints, but without traces of partitions; terminated on one side by an inflation, oftentimes with some interior partitions, and on the other by two tubes, distinct and sub-articulated.

S. arenaria. The Sand Septaria.
The type of this genus.

5. Teredina. Two fossil species.

A genus without a living species, given here to preserve the family entire, having a shell thick, oval, short, very gaping posteriorly, equivalve, inequilateral; summits well marked; a spoonlike cavity in each valve.

Tube or sheath testaceous, cylindrical; anterior end open; posterior end closed, but exhibiting the two valves of the shell.

6. Teredo. The Ship Worm. Three species.

This genus derived its name from the faculty it possesses of boring wood. The T. navalis can penetrate the stoutest oaken planks of a ship's sides by means of two valves affixed to the head of the animal. The effects produced would be much more destructive but from the fact of their generally perforating the wood in the direction of the grain. Sir E. Home wrote a very scientific and interesting description of a species not mentioned by Lamarck, called the T. gigantea, found imbedded in indurated mud in the Island of

Sumatra. It is the largest species known, some having been seen four or five feet long.

Shell thick, solid, very short or annular, open at both extremities; equivalve, equilateral, angular and sharp anteriorly, only slightly touching by the opposite edges; hinge obsolete; a considerable internal spoonlike cavity; one slightly sensible muscular impression.

Tube more or less distinct from the substance in which the animal lives, cylindrical, straight or flexuous, closed with age at the oral extremity so as to envelop the animal and its shell; always open at the other end, and divided interiorly into two syphons by a middle partition.

Teredo navalis.　　　　Teredo palmulata.
　　　　　T. gigantea.

T. navalis. The common Ship Worm.

Species very thin, cylindrical, and smooth; slightly twisted, white, finely striated longitudinally.

FAMILY II.
Pholadaria. Two genera.

1. Pholas. The Stone Piercer. Nine species.

This genus is without any tubular sheath; it derives its name from the Greek word φωλεω, to hide, alluding to the custom of its inhabitant in forming cells in rocks, wood, &c.

In form the Pholas is generally oblong, having two large valves opposite to each other, with a number of smaller ones attached to the back as a substitute for a hinge. The two large valves never shut close; they are open at one end, and sometimes at both.

The exterior of the shell is usually of a pure or dusky white, but sometimes of a brownish cast. In some species the shell is adorned with beautiful delicate reticulations, like the finest lace; in others the texture is coarser, like small basket-work. They are found in the American, Indian, and European seas, each shell in a separate habitation formed in limestone, sandstone, wood, coral, &c.; often discovered completely imbedded in the oak planks of ships traversing those seas; as they advance in growth they enlarge the space within, and leave the aperture by which they entered of its primitive size.

Shell thin, sub-transparent, finely striated, elongated oval, bivalve, equivalve, inequilateral; the valves only touching in the middle of their edges; the summits but little marked, and concealed by a callosity produced by the expansion of the dorsal lobes of the mantle; near the hinge are often developed one or more accessory calcareous pieces; an incurved tooth interior beneath the hinge.

Pholas dactylus.   Pholas silicula.
P. orientalis.   P. costata.
P. candida.   P. crispata.
P. dactyloides.   P. callosa.
          P. clavata.

P. dactylus. The prickly Pholas. Pl. 3, fig. 3.

Answers to the general description, but is beset with small calcareous spiny nodules on the ribs, which run widening and enlarging from the summit to the margin; colour white or very light brown.

P. striata. The striated Pholas. Pl. 3, fig. 5.

Oval, the dorsal callosity leaving the summit free, and extending towards the anterior and inferior extremity in such a manner that each valve seems to be formed of three parts, because of an oblique furrow from the summit to the margin; a tooth running down in the inside from the summit; one pair of accessory pieces at the posterior extremity of the shell.

P. candida. The white Pholas. Pl. 3, fig. 2.

Elongated, wedge-shaped; muscular impression almost medial; a kind of oblique tooth parting from the summit; no accessory pieces.

P. costata. The ribbed Pholas. Pl. 3, fig. 4.

Elongated, wedge-shaped, covered with regular elevated jagged or scalloped ribs, elegantly disposed; three dorsal accessory pieces; muscular impression almost medial.

P. crispata. The curled Pholas.

Somewhat oval, truncated behind, and as if divided into two parts by an oblique furrow from the summit to the base; anterior part reticulated, the other parts plain; muscular impression marginal.

P. clavata. The clubbed Pholas.

Short, wedge-form, little gaping, with many accessory pieces.

2. Gastrochæna. Three species.

Always without accessory pieces, and, therefore, easily distinguished from the Pholas.

Shell equivalve, somewhat wedge-shaped, with a very large, oval, oblique, anterior opening between the valves; the posterior extremity nearly close; hinge linear, marginal, without teeth; two distant muscular impressions; sometimes with a kind of tube or calcareous general envelope.

Gastrochæna cuneiformis. Gastrochæna mytiloides.
G. modiolina.

G. modiolina. The Modioliform Gastrochæna.

Oval, thin, brittle, gaping at the side; light reddish brown, with a bluish white interior.

G. cuneiformis. The wedgelike Gastrochæna. Pl. 3, fig. 1.

Species with a smooth shell, and without distinct tube. (Represented as imbedded in wood.)

FAMILY III.

SOLENIDES. Four genera.

1. Solen. Eighteen species.

There are many species belonging to this genus differing considerably in form and appearance. Its name is derived from a Greek word signifying a pipe or tube. It is a bivalve whose breadth sometimes exceeds its length; some species have a resemblance to the sheath of a razor or a knife handle; others are curved like the scabbard of a cimeter.

The Solen is found in the sand of the seashore, which it sometimes penetrates to the depth of one or two feet. Most of the species are covered with an epidermis, which renders their colours more or less obscure. In general they present but little beauty, though some are of a bright pink colour, and some are beautifully and delicately radiated with purple and white.

The principal characteristic of this genus is the hinge, which generally has one subulate tooth, though sometimes two or three.

Shell equivalve, extremely inequilateral, transversely elongated, open at both ends; the apices very small, and entirely at the commencement of the dorsal line; one or two teeth in the hinge; ligament external; two distant muscular impressions; the anterior one very long and narrow, the posterior one sub-angular.

Solen vagina.	Solen vaginoides.
S. corneus.	S. siliqua.
S. ensis.	S. cultellus.
S. pygmæus.	S. planus.
S. ambiguus.	S. minutus.
S. Dombeii.	S. constrictus.
S. Javanicus.	S. coarctatus.
S. Caribæus.	S. rostratus.
S. antiquatus.	S. violaceus.

S. vagina. The Razor Sheath. Pl. 31, fig. 5.

Valves equal, truncated at both ends; straight or slightly curved; summit terminal.

S. cultellus. The kidney-shaped Solen.

Species a little curved lengthwise; summit not terminal.

S. rostratus. The violet-beaked Solen.

Species with longer and narrower valves, flatter at the extremities; callosity at the hinge very visible; cardinal teeth or hinge nearer the middle than the anterior side.

S. ensis. The Sabre Solen.

Species linear, sabre-shaped; a single compressed tooth in each valve; olive brown at the base, and of a purple hue near the apex.

S. siliqua. The podlike Solen.

Species linear, straight; two teeth in one valve and one in the other; covered with a glossy brown epidermis; striated transversely.

S. antiquatus. The Antiquated Solen.

Species thin, white, and almost transparent; striated concentrically; ends rounded; hinge near the centre; a tooth in one valve locking into two in the other; the teeth erect and projecting beyond the margin; covered with a dark-coloured epidermis.

2. Panopæa. One species.

Distinguished from the Mya by the prominency of the apex and the situation of the ligament.

Shell regular, elongated oval, gaping at the two extremities, equivalve, inequilateral; summit but little marked, and anterodorsal; hinge very complete, similar, formed by a conical primary tooth before a short, compressed, ascending callosity; ligament exterior, attached to the callosity; two muscular impressions.

P. Aldrovandi. The Panopæa of Aldrovandus. Pl. 5, fig. 2.

The type of this genus, transversely elongated, undulated; concentrically wrinkled; of dark green colour, almost black.

3. Solecurtus. Three species.

Shell oval, elongated, equivalve, sub-equilateral, edges almost straight and parallel; the extremities equally rounded, and as if truncated; summits but little marked; hinge toothless, or formed by some rudimentary primary teeth; ligament projecting, affixed to the thick nymphal callosities; two distant, rounded muscular impressions.

Solecurtus radiatus.   Solecurtus strigilatus.
S. legumen.

S. radiatus. The radiated Solecurtus:

Species flat, small, with an interior ridge running down obliquely from the summit to the abdominal margin.

S. strigilatus. The strigilated Solecurtus.

Species more cylindrical, without interior ridge.

S. legumen. The Pease-pod Solecurtus. Pl. 31, fig. 6.

Species still more elongated and sub-cylindrical.

4. Glycimeris. Two species.

Distinguished from the Solen by being without teeth at the hinge.

Shell covered with epidermis, slightly irregular, elongated, gaping at the two extremities, equivalve, inequilateral; the summits but little marked; hinge toothless; a longitudinal callosity; ligament exterior, affixed to very projecting callosities on the shortest side of the shell; two distinct muscular impressions.

Glycimeris margaritacea.   Glycimeris siliqua.

G. siliqua. The podlike Glycimeris.

Transversely oblong, covered with a black epidermis;

umbones decorticated; internal disc of the valves white, thick, and callous.

FAMILY IV.
Myaria. Two genera.

1. Mya. The Trough Shell, or Gaper. Four species.

This term is derived from the Greek word $μυω$, to close, alluding to the animal's custom of closing the valves. The principal characteristic of the Mya is its gaping at one end; it is likewise distinguished by having a large spoonlike tooth proceeding from beneath the beak. Its form is greatly varied, but generally covered with a greenish epidermis, which may be removed; and the shell, when polished, will display beautiful prismatic colours. The Mya is found on the seashore or on the banks of large rivers, partially concealed in the sand and mud.

Shell transverse, inequilateral, surrounded with a thick epidermis; rather solid; edges thin and sharp; summits but little marked; hinge dissimilar; one or two large, compressed, spoon-shaped teeth rising perpendicularly from the plane of the left valve, and fitting into the entrance of a primary cavity in the right valve; ligament interior, attaching the tooth and cavity; two distant muscular impressions; the anterior long and narrow, the posterior rounded; the mantle impression narrow, with a large sinus or hollow.

    Mya truncata.   Mya erodona.
    M. arenaria.   M. solenimyalis.

M. arenaria. The Sand Mya. Pl. 5, fig. 1.
Regular species.

M. erodona. The Erodona Mya.
Irregular species, in which the cavity of the right valve is bordered by strong projections.

M. truncata. The truncated Mya. Pl. 5, fig. 3.
Sub-oval, truncated; small end gaping; large end round-

ed; covered with a dark yellowish epidermis; inside white; wrinkled transversely.

2. Anatina. The Duck's Bill. Ten species.

Shell elongated oval, very thin, fragile, semipellucid; much inflated at one end like a duck's bill, whence it derives its common name; equivalve, very inequilateral; hinge toothless; the anterior side rounded and much longer than the posterior; ligament interior affixed to a bony spoonlike process in each valve, and sustained by a lateral plate running obliquely into the interior of the shell.

Anatina laterna.	Anatina trapezoides.
A. truncata.	A. rugosa.
A. subrostrata.	A. imperfecta.
A. longirostris.	A. myalis.
A. globulosa.	A. rupicola.

A. subrostrata. The beaklike Anatina.
Species equivalve and regular.

A. myalis. The Mya-like Anatina.
Species inequivalve.

A. trapezoides. The trapezium-shaped Anatina. Pl. 12, fig. 5.

Species with a moveable tooth or calcareous piece upon the right valve, lodged in the angle formed by the spoonlike process.

FAMILY V.

MACTRACEA. Seven genera.

1. Lutraria. Eleven species.

This genus was taken from the Mactra, and is perfectly distinct, as it wants the lateral teeth. It is called Lutricola by De Blainville, from its lurking in sand or mud at the mouths of large rivers.

Shell inequilateral, orbicular, sub-triangular or transversely oval, gaping at the extremities; hinge with one cardinal tooth folded in two, or two teeth, one of which is plain, with an opposite hollow to receive it; no lateral teeth; ligament interior and fixed in the hollow cavity of the primary tooth.

<table>
<tr><td>Lutraria solenoides.</td><td>Lutraria elliptica.</td></tr>
<tr><td>L. rugosa.</td><td>L. papyracea.</td></tr>
<tr><td>L. compressa.</td><td>L. plicatella.</td></tr>
<tr><td>L. piperata.</td><td>L. crassiplica.</td></tr>
<tr><td>L. tellinoides.</td><td>L. complanata.</td></tr>
<tr><td colspan="2" align="center">L. candida.</td></tr>
</table>

L. solenoides. The Solen-like Lutraria.

Species oblong, sub-cylindrical, very gaping, two very strong cardinal teeth; the spoonlike cavity of the ligament vertical.

L. compressa. The compressed Lutraria.

Species oval or orbicular, almost equilateral, very compressed, little gaping; hinge similar; internal ligament inserted in the pit of a vertical spoonlike cavity; two distinct tubes, without longitudinal striæ.

L. rugosa. The rugged Lutraria.

Species ovate, closed at both ends; striæ from the summit to the base.

L. elliptica. The oval Lutraria.

Oblong oval, nearly smooth, having a few concentric striæ, and some diagonal striæ at the ends of the valves; colour yellow or greenish brown; inside white.

2. Mactra. The Kneading-trough. Thirty-three species.

The name given to this genus was derived from the Greek word μακτρα, from its resemblance to a trough used for kneading bread.

In all species of this genus a similarity of colouring and form pervades the whole. In shape they are sub-triangular or oblong, with a smooth, striated, or transversely-ribbed exterior. In some species the valves gape at both ends, and in others at the anterior only. The most general colour is lilach, or white tinged with blue or yellow; some have purple rays on a brown ground.

A singularity in the form of the hinge of the Mactra distinguishes it from all other genera. It is of a triangular form, has a bent or angular compressed tooth on each valve, with a small oblique cavity on each side to which the ligament is attached. There are also two lateral teeth, one near the ligament and the other near the primary tooth. These teeth are thin and fragile; the primary tooth is sometimes indistinct, but the lateral teeth always exist.

The Mactra is found buried in the sand at a little distance from the seashore. Shell generally thin and brittle, covered with epidermis, of a triangular form, transverse, equivalve, inequilateral; beaks prominent; one compressed, folded, cardinal tooth, with an adjoining pit in each valve, projecting inward; lateral teeth thin, lamellous, entering, placed near the hinge; exterior ligament small; an interior ligament inserted in the cardinal pits; two muscular impressions, united by a narrow marginal tongue.

Mactra gigantea.	Mactra Helvacea.
M. Spengleri.	M. grandis.
M. striatella.	M. stultorum.
M. carinata.	M. maculosa.
M. straminea.	M. ovalina.
M. Australis.	M. alba.
M. violacea.	M. solida.
M. fasciata.	M. castañea.
M. turgida.	M. rufa.
M. plicataria.	M. squalida.
M. rufescens.	M. Brasiliana.
M. maculata.	M. donacina.
M. subplicata.	M. depressa.
M. triangularis.	M. lilacea.
M. lactea.	M. trigonella.
M. abbreviata.	M. deltoides.

M. crassatella.

M. gigantea. The gigantic Mactra.

Species in which the cardinal teeth are almost obsolete, in consequence of the enlargement of the pit of the ligament.

M. stultorum. The fool's Mactra. Pl. 9, fig. 6.

Species in which all the teeth are very large, lamellous, striated longitudinally; colour reddish brown.

M. solida. The solid Mactra.

Species thick, solid, without epidermis; lateral teeth finely striated.

M. trigonella. The three-cornered Mactra.

Species in which the lateral teeth are almost obsolete; exterior surface smooth.

M. triangularis. The triangular Mactra.

Species very small, strong, opaque, white; inside white; margin strongly crenated.

M. crassa. The thick Mactra.

Species very thick, solid, striated longitudinally; the cardinal teeth obsolete, or almost so; the lateral very thick, very close, and reflected; an external ligament as well as an internal one.

3. Crassatella. Eleven species.

May be easily known from the Mactra and Lutraria, as the valves, when closed, fit exactly, and do not gape. It is remarkable that all the living species contained in this genus only exist in the seas of Australasia, while at least seven species in a fossil state are found in France.

Shell inequilateral, sub-orbicular, close, equivalve, sometimes attenuated at one end; two divergent primary teeth, with a cavity at the side; lateral teeth obsolete; ligament internal, inserted in the cavity of the hinge.

Crassatella Kingicola.	Crassatella subradiata.
C. donacina.	C. contraria.
C. sulcata.	C. cuneata.

C. rostrata.   C. erycinæa.
C. glabrata.   C. cycladea.
             C. striata.

C. sulcata. The furrowed Crassatella. Pl. 6, fig 4.

Shell ordinarily thick, striated transversely, denticulated, sub-triangular, equivalve, inequilateral, summits well marked and evidently turned forward; hinge very large, subsimilar, formed by two diverging cardinal teeth, separated by a large pit; ligament almost entirely interior, and inserted in the pit.

C. Kingicola. The King's Island Crassatella.

Ovate, orbicular; yellowish white, with obsolete rays; very minutely striated transversely; the umbones somewhat plicated.

4. Erycina. One species.

The only living species of this genus is found on the sand in New-Holland, but there are many fossils in France. It is so equivocal in character that it is difficult to judge of their hinge.

E. cardioides. The cardium-shaped Erycina. Pl. 6, fig. 5.

Shell rather longer than high, sub-triangular, regular, equivalve, inequilateral, rarely gaping; the summits well marked and a little anteriorly inclined; hinge subsimilar; two unequal cardinal teeth, converging at the summit, and leaving a pit between them; two lateral teeth, not distant, lamellous, inserted; ligament interior, fixed in the cavity between the primary teeth.

5. Ungulina. Two species.

This genus is very remarkable for having the pit or cavity divided into two parts, the one at the end of the other; the ligament is partially seen from the outside.

    Ungulina oblonga.   Ungulina transversa.

U. transversa. The transverse Ungulina.

Shell vertical or longitudinal, rather irregular, not gaping, equivalve, inequilateral, with summits little marked and decorticated; hinge dorsal, formed by one short, primary cleft tooth, before an oblong pit, divided by a small ligament, in which is inserted a sub-interior ligament; colour yellowish brown.

6. Solenimya. Two species.

This genus, which at first sight is confounded with the Solens, differs from them particularly by the singular disposition of the ligament placed at the short side of the shell.

Solenimya Australis.   Solenimya Mediterranea.

S. Australis. The Australian Solenimya. Pl. 6, fig. 2.

Shell covered with a thick brownish epidermis, regular, thick, elongated oval, edges straight and parallel, equally rounded at both extremities; valves equal, very inequilateral.

S. Mediterranea. The Mediterranean Solenimya.

Transversely oblong; dark brown, ribbed longitudinally, with imbricated projecting foliations; inside white.

7. Amphidesma. Sixteen species.

This genus was constituted by Lamarck on account of the peculiar characters which distinguished it from those genera which it most resembles; particularly in having the valves connected by two ligaments.

Shell generally small, transverse, suboval or rounded, occasionally a little gaping at the sides; hinge with one or two cardinal teeth, and a narrow cavity for the interior ligament; exterior ligament short.

Amphidesma variegata.	Amphidesma flexuosa.
A. donacilla.	A. prismatica.
A. lactea.	A. phaseolina.
A. cornea.	A. corbuloides.
A. albella.	A. glabrella.

A. lucinalis.	A. purpurascens.
A. Boysii.	A. nucleola.
A. tenuis.	A. physioides.

A. glabrella. The smooth Amphidesma. Pl. 6, fig. 9.

Species lenticular or oval, with or without a lunated depression.

A. lactea. The milky Amphidesma.

Sub-orbicular, sub-pellucid, compressed, reticulated; yellowish white.

FAMILY VI.

CORBULACEA. Two genera.

1. Corbula. Nine species.

This genus approximates the Crassatella and Ungulina, but is distinguished from them by the inequality of the valves and the strong primary tooth.

Shell rather solid, a little irregular and triangular, inequivalve, more or less inequilateral, rounded and enlarged before, attenuated and prolonged behind; summits well marked, one projecting behind the other; hinge anomalous, formed by a large, conical, recurved cardinal tooth, with a cavity at its base for the reception of the tooth of the other valve; ligament very small; two muscular impressions little distant.

Corbula Australis.	Corbula Taitensis.
C. sulcata.	C. nucleus.
C. erythrodon.	C. impressa.
C. ovalina.	C. porcina.
	C. semen.

C. nucleus. The kernel Corbula.

Strong, sub-triangular, under valve larger than the upper one; transversely striated; covered with a thick brownish epidermis.

C. ovalina. The ovate Corbula. Pl. 6, fig. 6.

Regular species.

C. Australis. The Australian Corbula.
Irregular species, living in stone.

2. Pandora. Two species.

Closely allied to the Corbula.

Pandora rostrata.   Pandora obtusa.

P. rostrata. The beaked Pandora. Pl. 6, fig. 3.

Shell white, regular, elongated, inequivalve, inequilateral; right or upper valve entirely flat, with a plait or fold; much produced towards the beak; hinge anomalous, formed by a transverse cardinal tooth on the right valve, entering into a corresponding cavity on the left; ligament internal, oblique, triangular, inserted in a pit rather deep, with edges a little projecting on each valve; two rounded muscular impressions.

FAMILY VII.

LITHOPHAGI. Three genera.

1. Saxicava. Five species.

This genus is taken from the Mytilus, and, like the Pholas, possesses the faculty of penetrating calcareous rocks, from which it cannot be extracted without breaking the substance in which it is imbedded.

Shell bivalve, thick, covered with epidermis, rather irregular, elongated, sub-cylindrical, obtuse at the two extremities; summits little marked; hinge toothless, or with a very small rudimentary tooth; ligament external, a little inflated.

Saxicava rugosa.   Saxicava pholadis.
S. Gallicana.   S. Australis.
       S. veneriformis.

S. Australis. The Australian Saxicava. Pl. 7, fig. 6.
Answers to the above description.

S. Gallicana. The Gallic Saxicava.
Oblong, wrinkled, truncated at the posterior extremity, one valve larger than the other; pale horn colour.

2. Petricola. Thirteen species.

This genus possesses the same faculty of boring rocks as the Saxicava; it is distinguished from the latter genus by the hinge having one or two teeth in each valve.

Shell sub-trigonal, transverse, inequilateral; upper side narrowed and a little gaping; lower side rounded.

Petricola lamellosa.	Petricola rocelaria.
P. ochroleuca.	P. exilis.
P. semilamellata.	P. ruperella.
P. lucinalis	P. chamoides.
P. striata.	P. pholadiformis.
P. costellata.	P. labagella.

P. linguatula.

P. lamellosa. The lamellous Petricola. Pl. 7, fig. 3.
Species oval, trigonal, radiated; two teeth on one valve, and one on the other.

P. pholadiformis. The Pholas-shaped Petricola.
Species transversely elongated.

3. Venerirupis. Seven species.

Another lithophagous shell, taken from the genus Venus, from which it is distinguished by the different disposition of the teeth, having three primary in one of the valves at least.

Shell more or less irregular, sub-trigonal, striated or radiated, equivalve, inequilateral, the anterior side shorter and rounded, the posterior sub-truncated; summits well marked; hinge sub-regular, more or less dissimilar, formed by slender, narrow, cardinal teeth, variable in number on each valve, sometimes two on the right and three on the left, and sometimes three on both; these teeth are small, contiguous, parallel, and but little, if at all, divergent exterior; very weak.

Venerirupis perforans.	Venerirupis exotica.
V. nucleus.	V. distans.
V. irus.	V. crenata.

V. carditoides.

V. perforans. The perforating Venerirupis.

Sub-rhombic, transversely striated, wrinkled on the anterior side; exterior brown, interior white, sometimes tinged with purple.

V. irus. The foliated Venerirupis. Pl. 7, fig. 2.

Species longitudinally striated; cardinal teeth two, sometimes three on the right and three on the left.

FAMILY VIII.
NYMPHACEA. Ten genera.

This family is divided into N. Solenaria and N. Tellinaria, from their resemblance to the Solen and the Tellina.

N. SOLENARIA. Three genera.

1. Sanguinolaria. Four species.

This genus may be distinguished from the Solen by never having the transverse oblong shape, or the edge of the valves parallel to the base.

Sanguinolaria occidens.	Sanguinolaria livida.
S. rosea.	S. rugosa.

S. rosea. The rosy Sanguinolaria.

Semi-orbicular, smooth, shining and convex; near the umbones of a beautiful rose colour, which becomes paler as it descends; acute transverse striæ.

S. occidens. The setting-sun Sanguinolaria. Pl. 7, fig. 4.

Oval, a little elongated, very compressed, slightly gaping, valves elliptical, equally rounded at the two extremities, without mark of posterior keel; summits slightly indicated; hinge formed by one or two contiguous cardinal teeth on each valve; ligament projecting, convex; margins not parallel.

2. Psammobia. Eighteen species.

Taken from the Tellina, which it much resembles in form, but from which it differs by not having the irregular plait on the anterior part.

Shell ovate, transverse, slightly gaping; summits projecting; hinge formed by two teeth on one valve, and only one inserted on the other.

Psammobia virgata.	Psammobia alba.
P. Ferroensis.	P. Cayennensis.
P. vespertina.	P. lævigata.
P. florida.	P. tellinella.
P. muculosa.	P. pulchella.
P. cærulescens.	P. aurantia.
P. elongata.	P. fragilis.
P. flavicans.	P. livida.
P. squamosa.	P. Galathea.

P. virgata. The striped Psammobia. Pl. 7, fig. 1.

Species rather gaping, striated longitudinally, the teeth of the hinge considerably effaced.

P. Ferroensis. The Ferro Psammobia.

Oblong oval; white, radiated with crimson; finely striated transversely; valves obliquely truncated.

3. Psammotæa. Seven species.

Of the same form as the Psammobia, but differing in the number of teeth, as the left valve of the Psammotæa has only one tooth; sometimes one valve is toothless, while the other has two teeth.

Shell transverse oval or oblong; gaping a little at the sides; one primary tooth on each valve, though sometimes on only one of them; ligament exterior, attached to callosities at the hinge, and without an irregular plait.

Psammotæa violacea.	Psammotæa serotina.
P. zonalis.	P. candida.
P. pellucida.	P. Tarentina.
P. donacina.	

P. violacea. The violet Psammotæa. Pl. 7, fig. 5.

Transversely ovate-oblong, sub-ventricose; transversely striated; purple radiations.

N. TELLINARIA. Seven genera.

The first five of these genera have one or two lateral teeth, the remaining two have none.

4. Tellina. The Tellen. Fifty-four species.

This genus differs but little from the Donax; its species are numerous, especially in the seas of hot countries; they are found sunk deep in the sand.

There are but few genera that can vie with the Tellina in beauty, variety, or number; some are smooth and polished, some are remarkable for their beautiful radiations, and others are covered with minute striæ and undulations; occasionally the whole surface is covered with imbrications or scales.

They are produced abundantly in almost every sea and in many rivers, but the finest species are found in the pearl-fisheries of Ceylon.

The usual form of the Tellina is broad at one end and gradually tapering towards the other. It derives its name from the Greek word τελειω, to bring to a termination.

Shell of variable form, generally striated longitudinally and very compressed; equivalve, more or less inequilateral; anterior side longer and more rounded than the posterior; offers a flexuous plait or twist at the inferior margin; summits little marked; hinge similar; one or two cardinal teeth; two distant lateral teeth, with a pit at their base in each valve; ligament external.

Tellina radiata.
T. unimaculata.
T. semizonalis.
T. maculosa.
T. virgata.
T. staurella.
T. crucigera.
T. Spengleri.
T. rostrata.
T. lutirostra.

Tellina elliptica.
T. albinella.
T. margaritina.
T. strigosa.
T. planata.
T. punicea.
T. depressa.
T. pulchella.
T. fabula.
T. tenuis.

T. sulphurea.	T. exilis.
T. foliacea.	T. donacina.
T. operculata.	T. nitida.
T. rosea.	T. scalaris.
T. chloroleuca.	T. psammotella.
T. remies.	T. striatula.
T. sulcata.	T. scobinata.
T. crassa.	T. decussata.
T. lævigata.	T. Brasiliana.
T. linguafelis.	T. obliqua.
T. rugosa.	T. umbonella.
T. lacunosa.	T. deltoidalis.
T. gargadia.	T. nymphalis.
T. pristis.	T. solidula.
T. multangula.	T. bimaculata.
T. polygona.	T. sexradiata.
T. capsoides.	T. ostracea.

T. radiata. The radiated Tellen. Pl. 8, fig. 5.

Shell elongated; posterior side shorter and more narrow than the anterior.

T. foliacea. The foliaceous Tellen.

Species transversely oblong; upon the edge of the front side of either valve are rows of serrated teeth, running from the apex to the margin.

T. bimaculata. The double-spotted Tellen.

Species orbicular, easily known by answering to its common name.

T. fabula. The false Tellen.

Shell very thin, pellucid, and oval; yellowish colour, darker towards the umbo, which is nearly central, pointed and turned a little to one side; anterior side slopes to an obtuse point; posterior side large and rounded; hinge with three teeth in one valve and two in the other.

T. scobinata. The rasp Tellen.

Species oval or sub-orbicular, sub-equilateral.

T. donacina. The Donax-like Tellen. Pl. 9, fig. 5.

Sub-oval, flattish, semi-striated and semi-pellucid; hinge with two teeth in one valve and one in the other; pale yellow, radiated longitudinally with pink.

T. depressa. The depressed Tellen.

Oval, flat, pointed at the smaller end and slightly reflected; pale yellowish colour, faintly striated concentrically; covered with a pale brown epidermis.

5. Tellinides. One species.

Though this genus bears a great affinity to many others, it cannot be united with any; having lateral teeth, it differs from the Psammobia; by not having the valves twisted, it differs from the Tellina; the valves closing, and having muscular impressions in the interior, render it distinct from the Lucina.

Shell equilateral, rather elongated, almost without the flexuous plait; two cardinal teeth diverging, and two remote lateral teeth, of which the anterior is but little distant from the summit.

T. Timorensis. The Tellinides of Timor. Pl. 8, fig. 3.

The only type and species of this genus.

6. Corbis. One species.

This genus was at first classed by Lamarck with the Lucina; but Cuvier, having discovered that the organization of the animals differed, made this a distinct genus, which was adopted by Lamarck.

Shell transverse, equivalve, no flexuosity; apices curved inward, opposed to each other; two primary and two lateral teeth, the posterior one nearest to the hinge; muscular impression simple, valves sometimes convex, strongly ribbed transversely, striated longitudinally, margins serrated and closely interlocking.

C. fimbriata. The fringed Corbis. Pl. 8, fig. 1.

Species white, rather thick, oval, a little elongated, almost equilateral; the cardinal and the lateral teeth well marked; the muscular impression anterior, rounded.

7. Lucina. Twenty species.

In the hinge and lateral teeth it much resembles the Tellina, but differs from it in never being flexuous. This genus is more easily characterized by the orbicular, compressed, general form of the shell, than by the dental system, which is sometimes entirely effaced.

Shell compressed, regular, orbicular, sub-equilateral; summits small and pointed, inclined anteriorly; hinge similar, but variable; two divergent cardinal teeth, little marked, and sometimes entirely effaced; two remote lateral teeth, with a pit at the base, sometimes obsolete; posterior ligament more or less sunk; two widely-separated muscular impressions, of which the anterior is narrow and long.

Lucina Jamaicensis.	Lucina concentrica.
L. Pennsylvanica.	L. divaricata.
L. edentula.	L. carnaria.
L. mutabilis.	L. scabra.
L. radula.	L. reticulata.
L. squamosa.	L. sinuata.
L. lactea.	L. pecten.
L. undata.	L. lutea.
L. circinaria.	L. digitalis.
L. columbella.	L. globularis.

L. Jamaicensis. The Jamaica Lucina. Pl. 8, fig. 8.

Species lenticular, striated concentrically; the teeth of the hinge variable, and sometimes obsolete.

L. undata. The waved Lucina.

Orbicular, thin, convex, undulated with fine irregular striæ; exterior pale yellow, interior white; margin glossy and plain.

8. Donax. The Wedge Shell. Twenty-seven species.

The singularity of form that gave rise to its common name renders it easily distinguished. It very much resembles a wedge, being very broad and thick at one extremity, and gradually tapering towards the other. They vary in colour, but the most general is purple radiated on a white ground, diverging from the beak to the margin; many have an orange tinge, and others a pink hue; the interior generally partakes of the colour of the exterior. There are not, perhaps, two species that have absolutely the same hinge.

The Donax is found buried deep in the sand of the seashore, with the short side uppermost.

Shell sub-trigonal, greater in length than in height, equivalve, very inequilateral; posterior side much shorter than the anterior; summits almost vertical; hinge complex, similar; two cardinal teeth in one or both valves; one or two remote lateral teeth on each valve; ligament posterior, short, and inflated; two rounded muscular impressions.

Donax scortum.	Donax granosa.
D. pubescens.	D. columbella.
D. compressa.	D. veneriformis.
D. cuneata.	D. Australis.
D. deltoides.	D. epidermia.
D. radians.	D. bicolor.
D. abbreviata.	D. vittata.
D. triquetra.	D. meroe.
D. ringens.	D. scripta.
D. rugosa.	D. trunculus.
D. Cayennensis.	D. flabagella.
D. elongata.	D. cinatinum.
D. denticulata.	D. Martinicensis.
D. cardioides.	

D. scortum. The beaked Donax. Pl. 8, fig. 4.

Species oval, of which the posterior side is sub-truncated; with decussated and muricated striæ.

D. trunculus. The common Donax.

Oblong, glossy, finely striated longitudinally, transversely banded and radiated with purple; white, clouded with purple within; internal margin of the valves distinctly dentated or crenulated.

D. denticulata. The denticulated Donax.

Species of which the posterior side is truncated; furrowed from the summit to the base.

9. Capsa. Two species.

This genus was separated by Lamarck from the Donax on account of the peculiarity of the hinge.

Capsa lævigata. Capsa Braziliensis.

C. lævigata. The smooth Capsa.

Triangular, sub-equilateral, obsoletely striated transversely; covered with a greenish yellow epidermis; inside violet towards the umbones.

C. Braziliensis. The Brazilian Capsa. Pl. 8, fig. 7.

Shell elongated, covered with epidermis; equivalve, close; the cardinal teeth reduced to one large sub-bifid tooth on the right valve, placing itself between two very thin ones on the left; ligament external, on the short side.

10. Crassina. One species.

Distinguished from the Crassatella by the position of the ligament, and from the Venus by having only two teeth on each valve; one of them on the left valve projects very slightly.

C. Danmoniensis. The Devonshire Crassina. Pl. 6, fig. 1.

Solid, thick, sub-orbicular, sub-equilateral; two very large divergent teeth on one valve, and two very unequal ones on the other; regular parallel grooves and ribs; covered with a yellowish epidermis; inside white; margin broad and plain.

FAMILY IX.

Conchacea. Seven genera.

This family is divided into Conchæ fluviatiles, fresh-water shells, and Conchæ marinæ, sea shells.

C. Fluviatiles. Three genera.

1. Cyclas. Eleven species.

The shells of this genus are very small, and are found buried in the mud of fresh waters; the apices or summits are never eroded, and some species are so thin as to be transparent.

Shell covered with a brown epidermis, oval or sub-orbicular, regular, equivalve, inequilateral; summits blunt, contiguous, or turned anteriorly; hinge similar, complex, formed by a variable number of cardinal teeth, and by two remote lateral teeth with a cavity at the base; ligament exterior, posterior, and convex; two distant muscular impressions, without posterior sinus.

Cyclas rivicola.	Cyclas obtusalis.
C. cornea.	C. fontinalis.
C. lacustris.	C. Australis.
C. obliqua.	C. sulcata.
C. calyculata.	C. striatina.
C. Sarratogea.	

C. cornea. The horny Cyclas. Pl. 9, fig. 7.

Species sub-orbicular, convex, thin, pellucid, with fine concentric striæ; cardinal teeth a little variable, always very small, and sometimes obsolete; summits not eroded, covered with a horn-coloured epidermis; interior bluish white.

2. Cyrena. Ten species.

This genus of shells is found in rapid rivers and streams; it was formerly classed with the Cyclas, from which, however, it greatly differs in having three cardinal teeth on each valve, and also lateral teeth. They are thick, solid shells, sometimes of a large size; the apices always eroded or carious.

Shell rounded and trigonal, ventricose, inequilateral; hinge with three teeth on each valve; two lateral teeth, one of which is near the primary ones; ligament exterior, placed on the largest side; in some species the lateral teeth are crenulated, in others they are entire.

Cyrena trigonella.	Cyrena fuscata.
C. orientalis.	C. fluminea.
C. cor.	C. violacea.
C. depressa.	C. Bengalensis.
C. Caroliniensis.	C. Ceylanico.

C. fluminea. The river Cyrena. Pl. 6, fig. 7.

Species sub-trigonal or elongated oval; summits decorticated, more anterior; three cardinal teeth, of which the two posterior are forked; exterior greenish brown, interior variegated with white and violet; sulcated transversely.

3. Galathea. One species.

This beautiful shell is found in fresh waters, and is distinguished from the Cyrena by the divergent form of the primary tooth.

G. radiata. The radiated Galathea. Pl. 6, fig. 8.

Shell equivalve, sub-trigonal, covered with a greenish epidermis, beneath which the surface is of a milky white, highly polished, with several violet or pale chestnut rays diverging from the apex to the margin; primary teeth furrowed, two on the right valve joined at the base, three on the other valve placed triangularly, the intermediate one being advanced, separate, thick, and callous; the muscular impressions are lateral, and appear double on each side.

C. MARINÆ. Four genera.
4. Cyprina. Two species.

This shell is generally large, resembling the Venus, from which it may be distinguished by having on the front side one impressed lateral tooth, which is sometimes obsolete; the nymphæ or callosities of the hinge large, arched, and terminated near the apices by a cavity, sometimes very deep.

De Blainville says that this genus is intermediary to the

Cyclas and the Venus, and contains but one living species; Lamarck makes two, though at first he characterized eight.

Cyprina tennistria.   Cyprina Islandica.

C. Islandica. The Icelandic Cyprina. Pl. 9, fig. 2.

Shell thick, regular, heart-shaped, covered with dark brown epidermis; white interior; sub-striated longitudinally; apices very strongly recurved anteriorly, and often contiguous; hinge thick, sub-similar, formed by three cardinal teeth but little convergent, and by one remote posterior lateral tooth, sometimes obsolete; ligament very thick, convex, fixed to large, arched, nymphal callosities, preceded by a cavity more or less deep, hollowed immediately behind the summits; muscular impressions sub-circular and very distant.

5. Cytherea.   Seventy-eight species.

This genus was taken from the Venus, and is easily defined as distinct from it by having four primary teeth on one valve, and only three united on the other, with an isolated cavity, oval and parallel to the margin; the lateral teeth divergent to the summit. In some species the internal margin is entire, having the anterior cardinal tooth with a striated canal or uneven sides; in others the anterior cardinal tooth is entire, without a striated canal; sometimes the internal margin is crenulated or dentated.

Shell solid, regular, equivalve, inequilateral; apices equal, recurved, and slightly projecting; four primary teeth on one valve, of which three are divergent and approximating at the base, and one remote; three primary divergent teeth on the other valve; with a distant cavity parallel to the edge.

Cytherea lusoria.   Cytherea graphica.
C. petechialis.   C. morphina.
C. impudica.   C. purpurata.
C. castanea.   C. casta.
C. zonaria.   C. corbicula.

C. meretrix.	C. tripla.
C. gigantea.	C. Venetiana.
C. erycina.	C. juvenilis.
C. lilacina.	C. rufa.
C. impar.	C. Guiniensis.
C. erycinella.	C. Dione.
C. pectoralis.	C. Arabica.
C. planatella.	C. trimaculata.
C. florida.	C. immaculata.
C. nitidula.	C. pellucida.
C. Chione.	C. hepatica.
C. maculata.	C. lucinalis.
C. citrina.	C. lactea.
C. albina.	C. exoleta.
C. lata.	C. lincta.
C. mactroides.	C. concentrica.
C. trigonella.	C. prostrata.
C. sulcatina.	C. interrupta.
C. Hebræa.	C. tigerina.
C. castrensis.	C. punctata.
C. ornata.	C. umbonella.
C. picta.	C. undatina.
C. tigrina.	C. pulicaris.
C. scripta.	C. mixta.
C. numulina.	C. abbreviata.
C. muscaria.	C. plicatina.
C. pectinata.	C. flexuosa.
C. gibbia.	C. macrodon.
C. ranella.	C. lunularis.
C. testudinalis.	C. squamosa.
C. divaricata.	C. lunaris.
C. cuneata.	C. cardilla.
C. placunella.	C. cygnus.
C. rugifera.	C. dentaria.

C. Chione. The Chione Cytherea.

Thick, solid, heart-shaped, covered with a smooth brown

epidermis, beneath which the shell is of a beautiful purple; radiated longitudinally, faintly wrinkled transversely, anterior cardinal tooth entire, and without a striated canal; apex turned sideways, with a cordiform depression.

C. mactroides. The Mactra-like Cytherea. Pl. 9, fig. 4.

Species thin, convex, triangular; summits very marked; margins sharp; anterior cardinal tooth entire.

C. pectinata. The pectinated Cytherea.

Species oval, thick, solid, more or less compressed, costated, pectinated upon the edges.

6. Venus.   Eighty-eight species.

This genus of shells is numerous and varied. It surpasses all bivalve shells in beauty, and is in form very like the Cytherea, but easily distinguished by the hinge, which almost invariably contains three approximate teeth, and a lateral tooth diverging to the summit. The internal margin of the valves is crenated or dentated, with or without lamellar striæ.

The shells are of the most beautiful and lively tints; the exterior as well as the interior colouring is of almost every possible shade and hue. They are found buried a little below the surface on the sandy shores of most parts of the world, particularly in warm climates.

Shell solid, thick, regular, perfectly equivalve and close, more or less inequilateral; summits well marked, inclined anteriorly; hinge sub-similar; the middle cardinal tooth forked, or three cardinal teeth more or less contiguous and convergent towards the summit; ligament thick, often arched, convex, and exterior; two distant muscular impressions; cordiform depressions beneath the beaks.

Venus puerpera.	Venus verrucosa.
V. reticulata.	V. rugosa.
V. pygmæa.	V. casina.
V. corbis.	V. crebiscula.

V. crenulata.
V. discina.
V. granulata.
V. marica.
V. cingulata.
V. cardivides.
V. grisea.
V. elliptica.
V. Dombeii.
V. mercenaria.
V. lagopus.
V. gallina.
V. gallinula.
V. pectinula.
V. sulcata.
V. lamellata.
V. exalbida.
V. rufa.
V. dorsata.
V. hiantina.
V. crassisulca.
V. corrugata.
V. Malabarica.
V. papilionacea.
V. adspersa.
V. punctifera.
V. turgida.
V. literata.
V. florida.
V. petalina.
V. bicolor.
V. floridella.
V. catenifera.
V. pulchella.
V. sinuosa.
V. tristis.

V. plicata.
V. cancellata.
V. pectorina.
V. sulcaris.
V. textilis.
V. texturata.
V. geographica.
V. rariflamma.
V. decussata.
V. pullastra.
V. glandina.
V. truncata.
V. retifera.
V. anomala.
V. galactites.
V. exilis.
V. scalarina.
V. Scotica.
V. aurea.
V. virginea.
V. marmorata.
V. ovulæa.
V. laterisulca.
V. callipyga.
V. opima.
V. nebulosa.
V. phaseolina.
V. carneola.
V. flammiculata.
V. conularis.
V. strigosa.
V. aphrodina.
V. Perronii.
V. aphrodinoides.
V. elegantina.
V. flammea.

V. rimularis.
V. vulvina.
V. vermiculosa.
V. subrostrata.
V. undulosa.
V. pumila.
V. ovata.
V. inquinata.

V. Casina. The Casina, or broad-ribbed Venus. Pl. 8, fig. 2.

Sub-orbicular, with transversely acute recurved ridges; lamellar striæ; crenulated on the hind margin; slightly channelled behind the depression.

V. decussata. The intersected Venus. Pl. 9, fig. 3.

Species sub-rhomboidal, with decussated striæ; margin not denticulated; umbo placed near one end; the three teeth of the hinge very contiguous and very weak; exterior brownish and marked with purple lines.

V. aurea. The golden Venus.

Sub-orbicular, inequilateral, transversely and concentrically striated; yellow golden colour.

V. corbis. The basket Venus.

Species sub-rhomboidal, deeply latticed; teeth very thick, ligament entirely concealed, margin dentated.

V. puerpera. The convex or spotted Venus.

Species thick, solid, orbicular or sub-orbicular, with concentric striæ, or, rather, laminæ; teeth very thick; margin dentated.

V. granulata. The granulated Venus.

Species thick, solid, cardium-shaped, radiated from the summit to the base.

7. Venericardia. One species.

This genus resembles the Venus, but has only two oblique cardinal teeth on each valve.

Shell equivalve, inequilateral, sub-orbicular, sides generally with longitudinal rayed ribs; hinge with two oblique cardinal teeth in each valve, turned in the same direction.

V. imbricata. The imbricated Venericardia. Pl. 9, fig. 1.

Species almost round, having convex longitudinal ribs, covered with imbricated rough scales; inferior margin rounded and dentated; more and more equilateral; the two teeth short and oblique.

FAMILY X.
CARDIACEA. Five genera.

1. Cardium. Cockle, or Heart Shell. Forty-eight species.

This genus received its name from its resemblance to a heart (καρδια). It is so well defined by Linnæus that no alteration was made by Lamarck, except in making two divisions of them; the first distinguished by having the anterior side as large or larger than the posterior, and no distinct angle at the apex; the second by possessing carinated or angular umbones, and the posterior side often much larger than the anterior. These shells are found at a small depth in the sand on almost every seashore.

Shell inflated, equivalve, sub-cordiform (when seen anteriorly), generally costated from the summit to the circumference; summits very evident; slightly recurved forward; hinge complex, similar, formed by two oblique cardinal teeth, articulating with the corresponding teeth on the other valve; two distant lateral teeth on each valve; ligament dorsal, posterior, and very short.

Cardium costatum.	Cardium Brasilianum.
C. Indicum.	C. apertum.
C. ringens.	C. papyraceum.
C. Asiaticum.	C. bullatum.
C. tennicostatum.	C. ciliare.
C. fimbriatum.	C. echinatum.
C. pseudolima.	C. lævigatum.
C. aculeatum.	C. biradiatum.
C. erinaceum.	C. eolicum.
C. tuberculatum.	C. pectinatum.

C. isocardia.	C. rusticum.
C. muricatum.	C. edule.
C. angulatum.	C. Groenlandicum.
C. marmoreum.	C. latum.
C. elongatum.	C. crenulatum.
C. ventricosum.	C. exiguum.
C. rugosum.	C. minutum.
C. sulcatum.	C. roseum.
C. serratum.	C. scobinatum.
C. unedo.	C. hemicardium.
C. medium.	C. cardissa.
C. fragum.	C. inversum.
C. retusum.	C. Junoniæ.
C. tumoriferum.	C. lineatum.

C. edule. The edible Cardium, or common Cockle. Pl. 10, fig. 2.

Species not gaping, with about twenty-six depressed ribs and transverse obsolete scales; of a cream colour; beaks protuberant.

C. cardissa. Venus's Heart.

Species heart-shaped, valves angularly flattened, umbones alternating.

C. lævigatum. The smooth Cardium.

Species smooth or nearly so, anterior side as large as the posterior.

C. hemicardium. The half-heart Cardium.

Species ribbed, with elevated rough striæ; the anterior side is very short and almost flat.

C. costatum. The high-ribbed Cardium.

No angle at the umbones; anterior side at least as large as the posterior; rows of white, hollow, elevated ribs, situated at regular distances, proceeding from the umbones to the margin, with the spaces between them of a reddish brown colour.

C. unedo. The Strawberry Heart.

Species with ribs armed with small crescent-shaped scales.

C. tuberculatum. The tuberculated Cardium.

Species not gaping, with large ribs armed with nodules.

2. Cardita. Twenty-one species.

Lamarck took this genus from the Chama on account of several peculiarities in the shell as well as in the animal. It is not affixed to other bodies by its lower valve, but, according to De Blainville, lies exposed on the rocks. There is some difficulty in distinguishing this genus from the Venericardia, without carefully examining the position of the two teeth.

Shell regular, thick, solid, equivalve, more or less inequilateral; summit dorsal, always very recurved anteriorly; hinge similar, formed by two oblique teeth; one short cardinal placed beneath the umbo, the other oblique, arched, marginal, and prolonged; ligament elongated, sub-exterior, and inserted; two very distinct muscular impressions.

Cardita sulcata.	Cardita intermedia.
C. ajar.	C. trepezia.
C. turgida.	C. bicolor.
C. squamosa.	C. depressa.
C. phrenetica.	C. concamerata.
C. crassicosta.	C. sinuata.
C. rufescens.	C. aviculina.
C. calyculata.	C. citrina.
C. subaspera.	C. sublævigata.
C. nodulosa.	C. corbularis.

C. lithophagella.

C. crassicosta. The thick-ribbed Cardita.

Species elongated, a little gaping at the inferior margin; ligament concealed.

C. sulcata. The furrowed Cardita. Pl. 10, fig. 3.

Sub-cordiform or oval, more transverse than longitudinal; colour white, tesselated with brown; posterior depression heart-shaped; longitudinal, convex, transversely-striated ribs.

3. Cypricardia. Four species.

Distinguished from the Cardita by having three teeth beneath the apices, and a callous lengthened tooth or ridge.

Shell obliquely elongated, equivalve, inequilateral; valves striated, but never ribbed; hinge with three teeth beneath the umbo, and one lateral elongated tooth.

Cypricardia Guinaica. Cypricardia rostrata.
C. angulata. C. coralliophaga.

C. Guinaica. The Guinea Cypricardia. Pl. 10, fig. 6.

Species elongated, very inequilateral; summit rounded and recurved anteriorly; two short divergent cardinal teeth, besides a lamellous tooth; ligament very long, projecting or not; yellowish white, covered with decussated striæ.

4. Hiatella. Two species.

Established by Daudin; classed by Linnæus with the Solen, but Lamarck is of opinion that it more nearly approximates the Cardita.

Shell thin, sub-rhomboidal, equivalve, very inequilateral, gaping at its inferior margin and posterior extremity; the summit very anterior and recurved in front; dorsal hinge formed by a single tooth on one valve corresponding to a semicircular slope on the opposite valve, or by a small tooth with a cardinal cavity in each valve; ligament probably exterior and dorsal; muscular impressions unknown.

Hiatella Arctica. Hiatella biaperta.

H. Arctica. The Arctic Hiatella.

Shell small, transversely oblong; apices truncated, with two divergent spring ridges; a small tooth on each valve; cream colour, with decussated striæ; inside pearly.

H. biaperta. The double-clefted Hiatella. Pl. 10, fig. 4.

Species that has only a single tooth on one valve; yellowish white.

5. **Isocardia.** Three species,

Taken from the Chama of Linnæus on account of a peculiarity in the shape of the cardinal teeth, and the singular curvature of the umbones.

Isocardia cor.   Isocardia semisulcata.
I. Moltkiana.

I. cor. The heart Isocardia. Pl. 12, fig. 4.

Shell free, regular, heart-shaped, equivalve, very inequilateral; summits diverging, strongly recurved spirally, forward, and outward; hinge dorsal, long, similar, formed by two flat cardinal teeth, with an elongated lateral one behind the ligament, which is dorsal and exterior, diverging towards the summits; muscular impressions very distinct and rather small; slightly wrinkled longitudinally; exterior reddish chestnut colour, interior white.

The Isocardia Moltkiana is a very rare shell, and the most elegant species of this genus.

FAMILY XI.

ARCACEA. Four genera.

1. **Cucullæa.** One species.

Distinguished from the Arca by the muscular impression within, to one side of which is an ear-shaped testaceous appendage; the shell is more trapeziform, and the hinge by age becomes obsolete, giving the teeth a more horizontal appearance.

Shell equivalve, inequilateral, trapeziform, heart-shaped; beaks distant, and separated by the angular groove of the ligament, which is altogether external; hinge linear, straight, with small transverse teeth, having at its extremity from two to five parallel ribs; valves marked with minute and strong longitudinal striæ, and sometimes one valve overlaps; margins crenulated.

C. auriculifera. The eared Cucullæa. Pl. 10, fig. 1.

Species navicular or obliquely heart-shaped, with decussated striæ; hinge completely straight, with two parallel ribs at each end, the terminal teeth longer and more oblique than the others; exterior chestnut colour, interior white, tinged with violet.

2. Arca. The Ark. Thirty-seven species.

This genus is easily known by its resemblance to the hull of a ship; the hinge is peculiar, being composed of numerous sharp teeth alternately inserted between each other. The Arca of Linnæus was divided by Lamarck into the four genera that compose this family, each possessing a strong distinctive character. All the shells of this family are found in the sea at a little distance from the shore; they are covered with a dark greenish lamellar or velvet-like epidermis, frequently ending in a deep fringe at the margin.

Shell a little varied in form, but most generally elongated, and more or less oblique at the posterior extremity; sometimes very inequilateral; summits more or less distant, and a little recurved forward; hinge anomalous, straight, or a little curved; long, and formed by a line of short vertical teeth decreasing from the extremities to the centre; ligament exterior, broad; sometimes the margin is crenated.

Arca tortuosa.	Arca barbata.
A. semitorta.	A. fusca.
A. Noæ.	A. Magellanica.
A. tetragona.	A. Domingensis.
A. umbonata.	A. lactea.
A. sinuata.	A. trapezina.
A. avellana.	A. pistachia.
A. cardissa.	A. pisolina.
A. ventricosa.	A. cancellaria.
A. retusa.	A. callifera.
A. sulcata.	A. irudina.
A. ovata.	A. bisulcata.
A. Helbingii.	A. Indica.
A. scapha.	A. senilis.

CONCHOLOGY. 63

A. antiquata.	A. Brasiliana.
A. rhombea.	A. corbicula.
A. granosa.	A. squamosa.
A. auriculata.	A. Cayennensis.

A. inequivalvis.

A. Noæ. Noah's Ark. Pl. 10, fig. 5.

Species boat-shaped, oblong, striated transversely and ribbed longitudinally; umbones remote and incurvated; margins entire and gaping; hinge straight; whitish, with divergent zigzag chestnut stripes; inside bluish white.

A. tortuosa. The twisted Ark.

A rare species; shell elongated, close, twisted; hinge completely straight.

A. barbata. The bearded Ark.

Species with the hinge straight, not hollowed or not gaping inferiorly, and of which the muscle is not adherent.

3. Pectunculus. Nineteen species.

This genus has the ligament partially inserted internally, and has no exterior angular groove. The valves never gape, often have rayed longitudinal ribs, are compressed, and the shell by age becomes thick and ponderous, sometimes attaining a large size. The teeth in the hinge are not so numerous as in the Arca and Cucullæa; the centre teeth appear worn down.

Shell close, orbicular, doubly convex, equivalve, sub-equilateral; summits almost vertical, and more or less distant; hinge formed on each valve by a rather numerous series of small teeth, disposed in a curved line, sometimes broken under the summit; ligament external and large.

Pectunculus glycimeris.	Pectunculus angulatus
P. pilosus.	P. stellatus.
P. undulatus.	P. pallens.
P. marmoratus.	P. violascens.
P. scriptus.	P. zonalis.

P. pennaceus.   P. striatularis.
P. rubens.   P. nummarius.
P. castaneus.   P. pectinatus.
P. pectiniformis.   P. radians.
P. vitreus.

P. glycimeris. The delicious Pectunculus.

Sub-orbicular, umbones produced; finely striated transversely and longitudinally; covered with epidermis, under which it is marked with reddish chestnut spots or bands; inside white; margins crenulated.

P. pilosus. The hairy Pectunculus.

Species convex, more or less smooth and hairy.

P. pectiniformis. The Pecten-shaped Pectunculus. Pl. 11, fig. 6.

Species lenticular, more compressed, pectinated, and more or less rough.

4. Nucula. Six species.

Shell small, more or less thick, sub-triangular, equivalve, inequilateral; summits contiguous and turned forward; hinge similar, formed by a numerous series of very pointed teeth, pectinated and disposed in a line interrupted under the summit; ligament internal, short, inserted in a small oblique cavity in each valve; two muscular impressions; valves more or less pearly within.

Nucula lanceolata.   Nucula Nicobarica.
N. rostrata.   N. obliqua.
N. pella.   N. margaritacea.

N. rostrata. The beaked Nucula.
Species of which the margin is entire.

N. margaritacea. The pearly Nucula. Pl. 11, fig. 7.

Species of which the margin is crenated; numerous regular pectinated teeth; obliquely ovate, trigonal; striæ minute and almost obsolete; covered with a greenish epidermis; inside silvery, pearl-like.

FAMILY XII.

TRIGONACEA. Two genera.

1. Trigonia. One species.

Supposed to be in very deep places in the sea; it is a strong, beautiful, pearly shell, sub-trigonal or sub-orbicular; thick, regular, equivalve, inequilateral; summits slightly prominent, recurved, anterodorsal; hinge complex, dorsal, dissimilar; two large oblong teeth laterally compressed, joined angularly under the summit, strongly furrowed on the right valve, penetrating into two excavations of the same form, equally furrowed on the left valve; ligament exterior and marginal; two distinct muscular impressions.

T. pectinata. The pectinated Trigonia. Pl. 11, fig. 4.

Species sub-orbicular, with radiated or divergent, prominent, and somewhat scaly ribs; inside pearly; margin crenulated.

2. Castalia. One species.

This genus is found in fresh waters, and differs from the Trigonia in the number and position of the lamellar teeth. The substance of the shell is pearly.

Shell sub-trigonal, equivalve, inequilateral; umbones eroded, covered with epidermis, and inflected anteriorly; hinge with two lamellar teeth, transversely striated, one of them posterior, distant, and shortened, the other anterior, lengthened, and lateral; ligament exterior.

C. ambigua. The ambiguous Castalia. Pl. 11, fig. 5.

Short, sub-trigonal; umbones truncated; longitudinally ribbed, with distant transverse striæ; covered with epidermis, under which the shell is of a pale chestnut brown, inside pearly; the lamellar and præ-apicial teeth are well marked, more regular, and all striated perpendicular to their length.

FAMILY XIII.

NAIADES. Four genera.

1. Unio. Forty-eight species.

The species of this genus become every day more numerous; they are found in all countries, but particularly in North America. The Unio is a fresh-water shell, and therefore, with great propriety, removed from the Mya, which consists entirely of marine shells. The substance is pearly; the exterior covered with a brown or green epidermis; the apices eroded. They are found in the mud of rivers, with their apices downward; some are slightly gaping, and some species produce fine pearls.

Shell generally very thick, pearly within, covered with epidermis; summits eroded, dorsal, and sub-interior; besides a long lamellous tooth under the ligament, the hinge is formed by a double precardinal tooth, more or less compressed, and dentated irregularly on the left valve, simple on the right valve; ligament external, dorsal, and post-apicial; muscular impressions well marked.

Unio sinuata.	Unio carinifera.
U. elongata.	U. Georgina.
U. crassidens.	U. clava.
U. Peruviana.	U. recta.
U. rariplicata.	U. naviformis.
U. pupurata.	U. glabrata.
U. ligamentina.	U. nasuta.
U. obliqua.	U. ovata.
U. retusa.	U. rotundata.
U. rarisulcata.	U. littoralis.
U. coarctata.	U. semirugata.
U. purpurascens.	U. nana.
U. radiata.	U. alata.
U. brevialis.	U. deladonta.
U. rhombula.	U. sulcidens.

U. rostrata.	U. luteola.
U. pictorum.	U. marginalis.
U. Batava.	U. angusta.
U. corrugata.	U. manca.
U. nodulosa.	U. cariosa.
U. varicosa.	U. spuria.
U. granosa.	U. Australis.
U. depressa.	U. anodontina.
U. Virginianum.	U. sub-orbiculata.

U. pictorum. The Painter's Unio. Pl. 8, fig. 6.

Species oval, not auriculated, strong, anterior side rhomboid and attenuated; the opposite side obtusely acute; the umbones somewhat warted; concentrically wrinkled; covered with a dusky green epidermis.

U. sinuata. The crooked Unio.

Species oval, sub-auriculated; cardinal tooth short, not lamellar or sub-striated.

U. sub-orbiculata. The sub-orbicular Unio.

Species round or almost round; cardinal tooth compressed, elongated, and often lamellar.

2. Hyria. Two species.

Easily distinguished from the Unio by a compound cardinal tooth, which slopes in an inclined position towards the posterior side. They are more found in lakes than in rivers.

Shell solid, pearly, equivalve, obliquely triangular, auriculated; base truncated and straight; hinge with two projecting teeth; the cardinal divided into numerous divergent parts; anterior ones smaller, the others long and lamellar.

Hyria avicularis.   Hyria corrugata.

H. avicularis. The little bird Hyria. Pl. 5, fig. 4.

Umbones smooth and polished; ears large, with pointed terminations; finely striated; interior pearly, exterior of a rich reddish golden-yellow colour; covered with a greenish brown epidermis.

3. Anodonta. Fifteen species.

A fresh-water shell, found in ponds and lakes, difficult to be distinguished from the Unio but by the hinge, which wants the cardinal and lateral tooth, and merely presents a smooth internal rim round the edge terminated by a sinus or notch, in which the anterior extremity of the ligament is sunk; the substance is pearly, covered with a false epidermis.

Shell ordinarily rather thin, regular, close, equivalve, inequilateral; summit anterodorsal; hinge linear, without teeth; ligament external, dorsal, and post-apicial; two well-marked muscular impressions.

Anodonta cygnæa.	Anodonta rubens.
A. anatina.	A. crispata.
A. sulcata.	A. uniopsis.
A. fragilis.	A. Pennsylvanica.
A. cataracta.	A. intermedia.
A. trapezialis.	A. glauca.
A. exotica.	A. sinuosa.

A. Patagonica.

A. cygnæa. The Swan Anodonta. Pl. 11, fig. 2.

Species oval, thin, elongated, hinge straight, and only auriculated anteriorly; beaks small and ventricose; concentrically wrinkled; covered with a greenish epidermis, which is frequently of a brown tinge towards the umbo.

A. rubens. The ruddy Anodonta.

Species oval, hinge arched, without trace of auricule or ear.

A. trapezialis. The trapezium Anodonta. Pl. 11, fig. 3.

Species oval or rounded, auriculated on both sides the summit.

4. Iridina. One species.

A very rare shell, separated from the Anodonta on account of the hinge being attenuated in the middle, and having small tubercles distributed along its length. The substance is thicker and more solid than the Anodonta, and of a brilliant rose-coloured pearly hue; it is found in the rivers of warm countries.

Shell equivalve, inequilateral, transverse, with small apices; recurved, but nearly erect; not auriculated; hinge very long, linear, crenulated through all its length; ligament external and marginal; two well-marked muscular impressions.

I. exotica. The exotic Iridina.

The only species of this genus answering to the above description.

FAMILY XIV.

CHAMACEA. Three genera.

1. Diceras. One fossil species.

Only found in a fossil state; distinguished from the Chama by the hinge, which is dissimilar, formed by a large thick tooth, concave in the greater valve; summits very projecting; almost regular spiral contortions.

D. arietina. The ram's-horn Diceras.

Shell irregular, inequivalve, inequilateral, somewhat heart-shaped, with divergent beaks.

2. Chama. The Clam or Gaper. Seventeen species.

In this genus are now comprehended only such as have a thick oblique transverse tooth, resembling a lengthened callosity, generally crenulated or grooved, fitting into a corresponding cavity in the lower valve. The animals inhabiting these shells have the faculty of affixing themselves to other bodies by the lower valve.

The Chama received its name from its gaping; it is found in most seas, particularly in the Southern; sometimes its colours are elegantly blended.

Shell irregular, adherent, inequivalve, inequilateral; summits more or less twisted spirally, especially in the lower valve; some from left to right, others from right to left;

hinge dissimilar, large, formed by one lamellous, arched, sub-crenulated, post-cardinal tooth, articulating into a furrow of the same form; exterior, post-apical, slightly inserted; two large and rather distant muscular impressions.

Chama Lazarus.	Chama florida.
C. damæcornis.	C. limbula.
C. gryphoides.	C. æruginosa.
C. crenulata.	C. asperella.
C. unicornis.	C. decussata.
C. arcinella.	C. albida.
C. radians.	C. ruderalis.
C. cristella.	C. croceata.

C. Japonica.

C. Lazarus. Lazarus's Chama. Pl. 12, fig. 2.

Species of which the summits twist from left to right; imbricated, dilated, waved foliations; striated obsoletely; exterior white, orange, red, or yellow; interior white.

C. arcinella. The hedgehog Chama.

Species of which the summits twist from right to left; the pink-coloured ones of this species are the most prized.

3. Etheria. Four species.

Distinguished from the Chama by the want of teeth in the hinge, and being of a pearly substance. It is a rare shell, only found in deep water, where it is attached to the rocks by the lower valve. Its irregular form is perhaps occasioned by the lower valve adapting itself to the form of the body to which it is affixed. Two species are fluviatile and two marine.

Shell adhering, irregular, thick, pearly, inequivalve, inequilateral; summits thick, little evident; hinge toothless, callous, thick, irregular; longitudinal, sub-dorsal ligament, partly exterior and partly penetrating into the shell; two oblong muscular impressions, one inferior and anterior, the other superior and sub-posterior; with or without an oblong incrusted callosity on the base of the valve.

  Etheria elliptica.   Etheria trigonula.
  E. semilunata.   E. transversa.

E. elliptica. The oval Etheria. Pl. 11, fig. 1.

Species with an oblong callosity on the anterior part of the shell; oval, depressed, dilated towards the umbones; summits distant.

E. semilunata. The semilunar Etheria.

Species without callosity at the base.

FAMILY XV.

Tridacnites. Two genera.

1. Tridacna. The Clamp Shell. Six species.

The most ponderous shell known, sometimes measuring several feet in length, and sometimes weighing five hundred pounds.

By Linnæus this genus was classed with the Chama, but the characteristic distinctions are so great that they are easily known. The Chama is irregular, has but one tooth, and is fastened to other substances by the lower valve; the Tridacna is equivalve, has but two teeth, and is affixed to other bodies by a byssus consisting of filiform tendons.

The animal inhabiting this shell is said to produce very fine pearls, but there is no pearly appearance on the valves.

Shell thick, solid, varying in size; some are very small and some very large; regular, triangular, more or less inequilateral; the summits inclined backward; hinge dissimilar, entirely anterior to the summits; one lamellous precardinal tooth, and two distant lateral teeth on the left valve, corresponding to two lamellous precardinal teeth and one remote lateral tooth in the right valve; ligament anterior, elongated; one forked sub-median muscular impression, almost marginal and oftentimes nearly obsolete; valves with broad, rounded longitudinal ribs, armed with vaulted scales, more or less elevated; posterior slope heart-shaped, and widely gaping.

Tridacna gigas.   Tridacna crocea.
T. elongata.   T. mutica.
T. squamosa.   T. serrifera.

T. gigas. The giant Tridacna. Pl. 12, fig. 3.

Species of which the shell is sometimes very large, white, transversely ovate or elongated; the anterior side longer than the posterior; broad ribs covered with vaulted scales; when of a pink or orange colour, greatly valued.

2. Hippopus. One species.

Similar to the Tridacna, but distinguished from it by having its posterior slope closed with a dentated margin; its ribs are never arched or vaulted, and its anterior side is shorter than the posterior side.

H. maculatus. The spotted Hippopus. Pl. 12, fig. 1.

Shell transversely ovate, ventricose, with scaly ribs; lunule, heart-shaped, and oblique; margins deeply crenulated; reddish purple spots.

FAMILY XVI.

MYTILACEA. Three genera.

1. Mytilus. The Muscle. Thirty-five species.

As arranged by Lamarck, now comprises only such shells as are regular, equivalve, and longitudinal; solid in substance, and attached to other bodies by a short thick byssus.

In colour and appearance they greatly vary, some being smooth and beautifully variegated with delicate colours, or radiated with purple and white; some are coarsely ribbed or granulated, and have only one colour, as black, blue, yellow, brown, or green; all are covered with an epidermis, to which oftentimes the colour is confined.

Shell of a close texture, elongated, more or less oval, sometimes sub-triangular, equivalve, summits anterior, more or less curved, a little sloping inferiorly; hinge generally without teeth, or with two very small rudimentary teeth; ligament dorsal, linear, sub-interior, inserted in a long and narrow furrow; two muscular impressions, of which the anterior is very small, with or without longitudinal grooves or furrows.

Mytilus Magellanicus.	Mytilus exustus.
M. erosus.	M. bilocularis.
M. crenatus.	M. ovalis.
M. decussatus.	M. ustulatus.
M. hirsutus.	M. Domingensis.
M. elongatus.	M. Senegalensis.
M. latus.	M. Afer.
M. zonarius.	M. achatinus.
M. ungulatus.	M. ungularis.
M. violaceus.	M. planulatus.
M. opalus.	M. borealis.
M. smaragdinus.	M. Galloprovincialis.
M. corneus.	M. angustanus.
M. edulis.	M. lineatus.
M. retusus.	M. lacunatus.
M. Hesperianus.	M. canalis.
M. perna.	M. incurvatus.

M. abbreviatus.

M. incurvatus. The incurvated Mytilus.

Nearly smooth, elongated oval, valves inflated and curved near the ligament; apex acute.

M. Afer. The African Mytilus.

More or less compressed and sub-triangular, without grooves; byssus very large and much developed; summit entirely terminal and anterior; smooth and radiated with blue or purple, covered with a dark brown epidermis; inside margin blue, shade decreasing to the centre.

M. crenatus. The crenated Mytilus.

Species longitudinally gooved, radiated, or striated.

K

M. hirsutus. The bearded Mytilus.

Species with grooves; covered with a shaggy or bearded epidermis.

2. Modiola. Twenty-three species.

Taken by Lamarck from the Mytilus, as it differs by being more transverse than longitudinal, and the beaks, instead of being terminal, are placed beneath the apex.

Shell smooth, sub-transverse, equivalve, regular, sub-triangular, the posterior side short; summits almost lateral; hinge lateral and linear, without teeth; ligament partly interior, placed in a marginal furrow; one sub-lateral elongated muscular impression in each valve.

Modiola Papuana.	Modiola Guyanensis.
M. tulipa.	M. Adriatica.
M. albicosta.	M. pulex.
M. vagina.	M. discrepans.
M. picta.	M. discors.
M. sulcata.	M. trapezina.
M. plicatula.	M. cinnamomea.
M. semifusca.	M. silicula.
M. securis.	M. plicata.
M. purpurata.	M. semen.
M. barbata.	M. lithophaga.

M. caudigera.

M. discors. The discordant Modiola.

Shell elongated oval, very convex, narrowest at the anterior end; striated at the two extremities; summit oblique; exterior greenish; interior white, with sometimes a pink tinge, and somewhat pearly; crenulated margin.

M. Papuana. The Papuan Modiola. Pl. 12, fig. 6.

Species smooth, more or less triangular; summit near the anterior extremity; byssus obsolete in adults.

M. sulcata. The furrowed Modiola.

Species striated longitudinally.

3. **Pinna.** The Wing Shell. Fifteen species.

This genus is the same as constituted by Linnæus; the shell is marine, generally very brittle and fragile, in form resembling an acute angled triangle; usually covered with longitudinal ribs and elevated transverse striæ; generally horn coloured.

This genus is remarkable for the production of an abundant byssus of a fine brown silky texture, which the Italians frequently fabricate into articles of dress, equal in appearance to the finest silk.

The Pinnæ often grow to a large size; they are sometimes found standing erect in the smooth-water bays, with the base of the shell uppermost, but generally affixed by the byssus to rocks and other sub-marine bodies. The filaments that compose the byssus are so tough and strong that the shells are not easily detached.

Shell fibrous, fragile, regular, equivalve, longitudinal, triangular, base gaping and as if truncated; summit pointed and straight; hinge dorsal, longitudinal, linear, and without teeth; marginal ligament occupying almost the whole of the dorsal edge of the shell; one very broad muscular impression behind a trace of the anterior in the summit.

Pinna rudis.	Pinna muricata.
P. flabellum.	P. pectinata.
P. seminuda.	P. saccata.
P. angustina.	P. varicosa.
P. nobilis.	P. dolabrata.
P. squamosa.	P. ingens.
P. marginata.	P. vexillum.

P. nigrina.

P. squamosa. The scaly Pinna.

Species very close and rounded at the posterior extremity; valves convex, covered with vaulted imbricated scales.

P. flabellum. The fan Pinna. Pl. 13, fig. 2.

Species gaping at the posterior extremity, which is as if

truncated; valves rather rounded at the upper end, and in the shape of an expanded fan; light fawn colour.

P. pectinata. The pectinated Pinna. Pl. 13, fig. 1.

Thin, pellucid; longitudinally ribbed and spinous for half its width, obliquely striated transversely on the other half.

FAMILY XVII.

MALLEACEA. Five genera.

1. Crenatula. Seven species.

There is one peculiar distinction between this genus and the Perna; the hinge of the Crenatula is composed of slightly concave callous crenulations, which receive the ligament; while in the Perna it consists of parallel truncated linear teeth (or, rather, riblike joints), corresponding and opposed to the opposite ones, the ligament being inserted only in their interstices.

Shell thin, very delicate, irregular, valves flattened, foliaceous, sub-rhomboidal, sub-equivalve; hinge longitudinal, dorsal, without teeth; ligament sub-multiple, and inserted in a series of rounded cavities corresponding with the dorsal margin; one sub-central muscular impression.

Crenatula avicularis.	Crenatula bicostalis.
C. modiolaris.	C. viridis.
C. nigrina.	C. mytiloides.
C. phasianoptera.	

C. avicularis. The avicular Crenatula. Pl. 14, fig. 2. Answers to the above description.

C. mytiloides. The muscle-shaped Crenatula.

Oblong, ovate, oblique; base acute; violet coloured, with obscure radiations.

2. Perna. Ten species.

In speaking of the Crenatula, we gave the characteristic distinction, which regarded it natural and expedient to make the Perna form a different genus.

Shell irregular, very compressed, foliaceous, sub-equivalve, rather variable form, gaping at the anterior part of the lower extremity; summit very small, hinge straight, vertical, without teeth; ligament multiple, and inserted in a series of longitudinal parallel furrows.

Perna ephippium.	Perna canina.
P. obliqua.	P. marsupiom.
P. isognomon.	P. sulcata.
P. avicularis.	P. vulsella.
P. femoralis.	P. nucleus.

P. femoralis. The femoral Perna. Pl. 14, fig. 1.
Species elongated, and with appendages like ears.

P. vulsella. The tweezer Perna.
Species elongated, without earlike appendages, or having very small ones.

P. ephippium. The saddle Perna.
Species round, compressed, very pearly in the interior; very slightly, if at all, auricled; margin acute; exterior purplish brown.

3. Malleus. The Hammer. Six species.

A shell of a singular form, resembling a pickaxe, found only in the Indian and Australian Seas; there are two species, the white and the black, both of which, when in fine preservation, are highly esteemed, but the white is more rare and valuable.

Shell sub-nacreous, irregular, rugged, sub-equivalve, inequilateral, generally auricled before and prolonged behind, so as to be in form like a hammer; summit entirely anterior; between them and the inferior auricle, an oblique cut or slope for the passage of the byssus; hinge linear, elongated, without teeth; ligament simple, triangular, inserted in a conical oblique cavity, partly exterior; one rather large sub-central muscular impression.

Malleus albus.   Malleus vulsellatus.
M. vulgaris.   M. anatinus.
M. normalis.   M. decurtatus.

M. vulgaris. The common Malleus. Pl. 14, fig, 4.

Species with two earlike appendages; trilobate, colour blackish brown.

M. albus. The white Malleus.

Species trilobate; base of the lateral lobe prolonged, without a sinus; the base and the pit of the ligament not distinct; colour white, with transverse undulations.

M. vulsellatus. The tweezer Malleus.
Species slightly auricled.

M. normalis. The square Malleus.
Species without earlike appendages.

4. Avicula. Thirteen species.

Remarkable for the form of its shell, which resembles, when partially expanded, a bird flying.

Shell foliaceous or not, thin and very fragile, always pearly, sub-equivalve; form sub-regular, but rather variable; summit anterior; valves oblique, the left one with a little notch, through which the byssus passes; sometimes unequally and obliquely auricled; hinge linear, toothless, or with two small rudimentary teeth; ligament more or less exterior, placed in a narrow groove, sometimes enlarged towards the summit; one very large posterior muscular impression; and one very small anterior.

Avicula macroptera.   Avicula Tarentina.
A. lotorium.   A. Atlantica.
A. semi-sagitta.   A. squamulosa.
A. heteroptera.   A. papilionacea.
A. falcata.   A. costellata.
A. crocea.   A. physoides.
          A. virens.

A. macroptera. The rounded Avicula. Pl. 14, fig. 3.

Species oval, oblique, the earlike appendages very developed, especially the superior; one tooth at the hinge.

A. Atlantica. The Atlantic Avicula.

Obliquely curved, yellowish fawn colour, with dark reddish-brown stains; interior pearly.

5. Meleagrina. Two species.

The form of the shell is orbicular and equivalve, without the elongated transverse base on the cardinal tooth, and the sloping sides of the opening for the passage of the byssus are perceptible on both valves; these peculiarities distinguish it from the Avicula.

Shell sub-equivalve, rotundate, nearly square, externally squamose; the inferior cardinal margin straight, not caudate anteriorly; a sinus at the posterior base of the valves for the passage of the byssus; the left valve being at this place narrow and channelled; hinge linear, without teeth.

Meleagrina margaritifera.   Meleagrina albina.

M. margaritifera. The pearl-bearing Meleagrina, sometimes called the mother-of-pearl oyster.

Species slightly oblique, somewhat square, pearly, very thick, compressed; undulated and transversely striated, with a series of lamellated longitudinal scales; exterior greenish, interior pearly. This shell is celebrated for its irridescent colours, and is valued for the beautiful and costly pearls it produces. These pearls are formed from a deposition of the substance destined to line the shell upon sand or other bodies, casually or purposely introduced within the mantle of the animal; the shell itself is the mother-of-pearl used for inlaying, or making various elegant trinkets.

FAMILY XVIII.

PECTINIDES. Seven genera.

1. Pedum. The Shepherd's Crook. One species.

The common name was given to this genus from the resemblance to a French shepherd's crook. The shell is of a regular form; its lower valve, in which is a sinus for the byssus, is turned up at the edges, and the upper valve falls within it.

Shell inequivalve, a little eared; apices unequal, distant, rounded, little evident; hinge without teeth; ligament inserted in an oblique groove, prolonged to the summit, and carried within in a kind of spoonlike cavity.

P. spondyloideum. The spondylus-shaped Pedum. Pl. 15, fig. 5.

Ovate, wedge shaped, flat; superior valve with longitudinal striæ; white, granulated, and rough; slightly tinged with purple near the beak.

2. Lima. The File Shell. Six species.

No sinus or notch; the valves, thick and gaping, form a lateral opening; the ears are small, but distinct.

Shell oval, more or less oblique, almost equivalve, with small ears, regularly gaping at the anterior part of the lower edge; summits anterior and distant; hinge longitudinal, without teeth; ligament rounded, almost exterior, inserted in a cavity of each valve; central muscular impression divided into three very distinct parts.

Lima inflata.	Lima annulata.
L. squamosa.	L. fragilis.
L. glacialis.	L. linguatula.

L. squamosa. The scaly Lima. Pl. 15, fig. 3.

Answers to the above description, with valves ventricose, armed with vaulted scales.

L. fragilis. The fragile Lima.

Oblong ovate, very pellucid, delicately white, with longitudinal distinct striæ; lower margin denticulated, closely interlocking when the valves are closed.

3. Pecten. The Scallop. Fifty-nine species.

The shells constituting this genus are found in all seas; they are well known, and many of them are very beautiful.

The form is usually regular; their surface is adorned with elevated divergent ribs, varying in number from five to thirty, proceeding from the beaks and terminating at the margins in a scalloped outline.

Some are equivalve, others have one valve flat and the other convex; the colours of the upper valve are brighter than those of the lower.

There is considerable variation in the size and form of the ears, which in some species are equal or nearly so, but in others are unequal; some are so small as to be nearly indistinct. The ribs are variously diversified with beautiful colours and delicate checker-work; the margins are mostly crenated, and oftentimes beautifully coloured.

These shells were formerly worn by Pilgrims on their hat or coat, as a mark of having been to the holy shrine in Palestine.

Shell free, regular, thin, solid, auricled, equivalve, equilateral; summits contiguous; hinge without teeth; a ligamental membrane through all the length of the hinge, besides a short, thick ligament, almost entirely internal, which fills a triangular cavity under the summits; one sub-central muscular impression.

Pecten maximus.	Pecten rastellum.
P. medius.	P. turgidus.
P. Jacobæus.	P. flagellatus.
P. bifrons.	P. aspersus.
P. ziezac.	P. flavidulus.
P. Latirentii.	P. plica.

P. pleuronectes.	P. glaber.
P. obliteratus.	P. sulcatus.
P. Japonicus.	P. virgo.
P. Magellanicus.	P. unicolor.
P. purpuratus.	P. griseus.
P. lineolaris.	P. distans.
P. radula.	P. Isabella.
P. nodosus.	P. lineatus.
P. pallium.	P. flabellatus.
P. pes-felis.	P. irradians.
P. tigris.	P. flexuosa.
P. imbricatus.	P. dispar.
P. histrionicus.	P. quadriradiatus.
P. sauciatus.	P. Islandicus.
P. opercularis.	P. inflexus.
P. asperrimus.	P. pellucidus.
P. senatorius.	P. Tranquebaricus.
P. aurantius.	P. gibbus.
P. florens.	P. miniaceus.
P. varius.	P. pusio.
P. sanguineus.	P. hybridus.
P. sinuosus.	P. sulphureus.
P. ornatus.	P. lividus.

P. glaber. The glabrous Scallop. Pl. 15, fig. 4.

Species of which the two valves are ribbed and almost equally convex, the right a little less, and having its inferior ear less broad than the left, so as to produce a kind of groove for the passage of the byssus.

P. Jacobæus. The scallop of St. James.

Species very inequivalve; the left valve being very flat, the right convex; ears equal.

P. pleuronectes. The sole Scallop.

Species equivalve, not closing; surface smooth and ribbed within; one valve perfectly white, the other of a brownish or reddish colour.

4. Plagiostoma. Ten fossil species.

Only known as fossils; probably introduced here by Lamarck to serve as a connecting link for the genera Lima, Pecten, Spondylus, and Podopsis.

Shell rather thick, regular, free, sub-equivalve, sub-auriculated; the two valves almost equally convex, both provided with a distinct summit, recurved in the middle of a level surface, with a great triangular slope in the middle; the cardinal base transverse, straight; hinge without teeth; a conical cardinal pit situated below the beak, partly internal, opening outward, and receiving the ligament.

P. spinosa. The thorny Plagiostoma.

Subarcuated, the umbo of one shell higher than that of the other, with longitudinal ribs and remote concentric rings.

5. Plicatula. Five species.

Separated from the Spondylus of Linnæus on account of its distinct structure. The ligament is altogether internal; it is without ears, and the prolonged beak so conspicuous in that genus. The Plicatula has the faculty of affixing itself to another body, so that many are found grouped together in clusters. The valves are strongly plaited within and without, closely interlocking with each other.

Shell solid, adhering, sub-irregular, without ears, inequivalve, pointed at the summit, rounded and plaited behind; hinge with two strong teeth in each valve, with a cavity between them, in which the ligament is internally inserted.

Plicatula ramosa.   Plicatula cristata.
P. depressa.   P. reniformis.
           P. Australis.

P. ramosa. The branched Plicatula. Pl. 15, fig. 2.

Oblong, trigonal, very thick; strong longitudinal plaits; exterior brown, with a yellow tinge, with reddish arrow-shaped markings; interior white.

6. Spondylus. The thorny Oyster. Twenty-one species.

The valves of this genus greatly resemble those of the common oyster, but have ears, and are covered with long recurved or straight-pointed spines.

The lower valve is much larger than the upper, and has foliaceous laminæ, by which it is attached to the other substances. They are found in all seas of hot countries, but particularly in the Indian; they adhere to rocks, coral, &c., oftentimes in large groups.

The usual colours are red, purple, white, brown, or orange, several of which are sometimes blended in the same shell.

Shell solid, adhering, sub-regular, more or less spined, sub-auriculated, inequivalve; the right or inferior valve fixed, much more excavated than the other, and having behind, at the summit, a triangular face, which enlarges and elongates with age; hinge longitudinal, provided in each valve with two strong teeth entering into corresponding cavities; ligament short, almost medial, partly exterior; one sub-dorsal, muscular impression.

Spondylus gædaropus.	Spondylus costatus.
S. Americanus.	S. variegatus.
S. arachnoides.	S. longispineus.
S. candidus.	S. regius.
S. multilamellatus.	S. avicularis.
S. coccineus.	S. microlepos.
S. crassisquama.	S. croceus.
S. spathuliferus.	S. aurantius.
S. ducalis.	S. radians.
S. longitudinalis.	S. zonalis.
S. violacescens.	

S. gædaropus. The thorny red Spondylus. Pl. 15, fig. 1.

Upper valve red, under one white, with longitudinal striæ or ribs; rough granulations, and somewhat tongue-shaped; rather short truncated spines.

S. longispineus. The long-spined Spondylus.

Thickly spined, longitudinally sulcated and ribbed; alternate spines arcuated and tongue-shaped; valves of a reddish colour; umbones orange.

7. Podopsis. Two fossil species.

Only introduced here to fill up the family and keep up the chain of connexion. It approximates the genus Gryphea.

Shell rather thick, sub-regular, symmetrical, equilateral, inequivalve, adhering by the extremity of the shorter valve; the other terminated by a summit pointed, a little recurved and medial; articulation very angular, by means of two very distant condyles.

FAMILY XIX.

OSTRACEA, Six genera.

1. Gryphæa. One species.

This genus resembles the Ostrea, with which it was formerly classed, but from which it is distinguished by the peculiar character of the lower valve. It is very deep and carinated, with a summit terminating in a long spirally recurved beak, slightly turned to one side; the edge sharp and angular.

It is seldom, if ever, attached to other bodies. Shell more finely lamellated than that of the oyster, free or slightly adherent, sub-equilateral, very inequivalve; the lower valve very concave, with a summit more or less recurved like a hook; the upper valve much smaller, and formed like a lid; hinge without teeth; ligament inserted in an oblong arched cavity; one single muscular impression on each valve.

G. angulata. The angulated Gryphæa. Pl. 16, fig. 2.

Oblong ovate, with three long longitudinal carinated ribs below; summit of the inferior valve is subvolute. This is a rare shell.

2. Ostrea. The Oyster. Forty-eight species.

As given by Lamarck, is a natural and well-defined family. It is too well known to require description. It fixes itself to other bodies by the laminæ of the whole surface of one valve, and generally remains immoveable, exhibiting no other signs of life than that of opening its valves to receive nutriment.

Shell irregular, inequivalve, inequilateral, exterior roughly foliaceous, interior somewhat pearly; the left or inferior valve larger, deeper, and adhesive, its summit prolonging with age in a sort of heel; the right or superior valve smaller, more or less in the form of a lid; hinge without teeth; ligament short, sub-interior, inserted in an oblong cardinal cavity, increasing with the summit; muscular impression single and sub-central.

Ostrea edulis.	Ostrea ruscuriana.
O. hippopus.	O. Virginica.
O. borealis.	O Canadensis.
O. Adriatica.	O. excavata.
O. cochlear.	O. mytiloides.
O. cristata.	O. sinuata.
O. gallina.	O. trapezina.
O. numisma.	O. tuberculata.
O. lingua.	O. rufa.
O. tulipa.	O. margaritacea.
O. Brasiliana.	O. gibbosa.
O. scabra.	O. Australis.
O. rostralis.	O. elliptica.
O. parasitica.	O. haliotidæa.
O. denticulata.	O. deformis.
O. spathulata.	O. fucorum.
O. cornucopiæ.	O. plicatula.
O. cucullata.	O. glaucina.
O. doridella.	O. fusca.
O. rubella.	O. turbinata.
O. limacella.	O. cristagalli.

O. erucella.	O. imbricata.
O. folium.	O. hyotis.
O. labrella.	O. radiata.

O. edulis. The eatable Oyster. Pl. 16; fig. 5.

Species orbicular, and not plaited; rugged, with undulated, imbricated scales; one valve flat and the other convex; variable in size; outside greenish brown, inside pearly white, sometimes with a bluish tinge.

O. Virginica. The Virginian Oyster.
Species longitudinal and not plaited.

O. imbricata. The imbricated Oyster.
Species orbicular and plaited.

O. crista-galli. The Cock's-comb Oyster.
Species strongly plaited longitudinally.

3. Vulsella. The Tweezers. Six species.

This genus has several characteristics which distinguish it from the Ostrea; they are free; the valves and the apices are nearly equal, with a projecting callosity on each valve, depressed underneath, and obliquely arched for the reception of the ligament.

Shell sub-nacreous, sub-regular, sub-equivalve, inequilateral; upper valve finely granulated, or striated longitudinally from the apex to the margin; summits anterior, distant, recurved below; hinge without teeth; ligament undivided, thick, inserted in a rounded cavity, made in a slightly projecting callosity on each valve; muscular impression subcentral, rather large, and two very small ones entirely anterior.

V. lingulata. The tongue-like Vulsella. Pl. 15, fig. 6.

Elongated, depressed, transversely striated; pale yellowish brown, with longitudinal darker stripes.

4. Placuna. The Chinese Window Shell. Three species.

This genus received its common name from the thin, transparent nature of the valves of the shell, particularly of the species *placenta*, which by the ingenious Chinese are often polished and used as a substitute for window-glass.

The hinge of the shells of this genus is so peculiar as to make it perfectly distinct; entirely interior, fastened by a ligament shaped like a V on one of the valves.

Shell free, sub-irregular, very thin, almost entirely transparent, flat, sub-equivalve, sub-equilateral, slightly auricled; hinge entirely internal, formed on the superior less valve by two elongated, unequal, oblique ribs converging at the summit, to the interior side of which a ligament like the letter V is inserted in two equally converging, rather deep cavities of the lower valve, which is more convex; one rather small, sub-central muscular impression.

P. placenta. The glassy Placuna. Pl. 16, fig. 3.

Sub-orbicular, flat, white, and transparent; finely striated longitudinally, slightly decussated.

5. Anomia. The Antique Lamp. Six species.

When Linnæus formed this genus and named it Anomia, he probably did so from its having no determinate character. Its common name was given it by the fancied resemblance of some of its species to an antique lamp. Like the oyster, they seldom leave their place; they are always affixed to marine bodies by an osseous operculum, formed by the thick extremity of the animal's muscle. The lower valve is perforated and smaller, conforming to the shape of the substance to which it is affixed.

Shell adhering, irregular, inequivalve, inequilateral, ostraceous; inferior valve rather more flat than the superior, divided at the summit into two sloping branches, whose approaching together forms a large oval hole, through which protrudes a muscle, the extremity of which becomes ossified and adheres to extraneous bodies; one sub-central muscular impression divided into three.

Anomia ephippium.	Anomia pyriformis.
A. patellaris.	A. fornicata.
A. cepa.	A. membranacea.
A. electrica.	A. squamula.
	A. lens.

A. ephippium. The Saddle Anomia. Pl. 16, fig. 1.

Shell sub-orbicular, irregularly wrinkled and waved; upper valve convex, under flat and perforated at the hinge, through which passes the ligament by which it is affixed to other bodies; inside pearly, and of various changing colours, such as green, purple, violet, and yellow.

6. Crania. The Scull. One species.

So called from the appearance caused by three holes or cavities on the surface of the lower valve.

Shell irregular, orbicular, inequivalve; the inferior valve almost flat, and marked on the interior with four muscular impressions, sometimes very deep, and of which the two sub-central are sufficiently connected to form but one; the superior valve like a Patella, more or less convex, with four very distinct muscular impressions, rather distant.

C. personata. The masked Crania. Pl. 16, fig. 4.

Orbicular; upper valve gibbous and conical, lower valve flat, with three perforations.

FAMILY XX.

BRACHIOPODA. Three genera.

1. Orbicula. One species.

Greatly resembling a Patella, for which it is often mistaken on account of the lower valve being very thin, flat, and adhering.

Shell sub-orbicular, very compressed, inequilateral, very inequivalve; the inferior valve very thin, adherent, and im-

M

perforated; the superior valve like a Patella, with a summit more or less inclined towards the posterior side.

O. Norwegica. The Norwegian Orbicula. Pl. 17, fig. 4.

Upper valve in the form of a depressed cone, with a summit produced and pointed.

2. Terebratula. Twelve species.

Taken from the Anomia, and with great propriety, as its characteristic differences are very great; the perforation of the Anomia is always in the smaller valve, which is attached to the larger by a cardinal ligament, while in the Terebratula the perforation is always in the larger valve, which is connected to the smaller by teeth at the hinge. In some the valves are smooth, and in others grooved longitudinally.

Shell thin, equilateral, sub-triangular, inequivalve; one of the valves larger and more convex than the other, prolonged behind by a sort of heel, sometimes recurved, and pierced by a round hole at its extremity; frequently sloped more or less by a cleft of variable form; the opposite valve smaller, more flat, sometimes formed like a lid, having in the interior a system of support variable in form and complication in every true species; hinge limited, prominent, and formed by two articulating surfaces of one valve placed between corresponding projections of the other; a kind of tendinous ligament issuing from the sloping cleft of the shell, by which it is attached to marine bodies.

Terebratula vitrea.	Terebratula pisum.
T. dilatata.	T. globosa.
T. rotunda.	T. sanguinea.
T. flavescens.	T. caput-serpentis.
T. dentata.	T. truncata.
T. dorsata.	T. psittacea.

T. dorsalis. The dorsal Terebratula. Pl. 17, fig. 1.

The summit of the large valve pierced with a round hole, very circumscribed; grooved longitudinally; valves as if cut sloping in the middle line.

T. globosa. The globose Terebratula.

Species smooth, with the valves rounded at their anterior edge.

T. caput serpentis. The Serpent's-head Terebratula.

Species grooved, with the summit or heel of the large valve deeply hollowed even to the edge of the articulation; the slope rounded; the valves sub-bilobate by the apparent slope of the anterior edge.

3. Lingula. One species.

The valves of this genus are united by means of a tubular, fleshy, or membranous peduncle surrounding the narrow part of them, and of which the base is affixed to marine substances.

Shell covered with epidermis, sub-equivalve, equilateral, depressed, elongated, truncated anteriorly, summit middle and posterior, without trace of ligament, but supported at the extremity of a long fibro-gelatinous peduncle, which attaches it vertically to sub-marine bodies; multiple muscular impression.

L. anatina. The Duck's-bill Lingula. Pl. 17, fig. 2.

Covered with a green, shining epidermis, shaped like a duck's bill, and having a cylindrical peduncle.

CLASS IV.

MOLLUSCA.
TWENTY-TWO FAMILIES.

FAMILY I.
PTEROPODA. Six genera

Some genera of this family are without a testaceous covering, and are mentioned only for the sake of preserving the family entire.

1. Hyalæa. Venus's Chariot. Two species.

This genus derives its common name from a fancied resemblance to a miniature triumphal car.

Shell very thin, transparent, symmetrical, convex below, flat above, valves unequal, form tricuspidated, cleft at the sides, open like a cleft anteriorly, and tridentated posteriorly; summit truncated.

Hyalæa tridentata.   Hyalæa cuspidata.

H. tridentata. The three-toothed Hyalæa.
Transparent, horn-coloured, globular; tridentated posteriorly; summit and two posterior sides open; finely striated transversely.

2. Clio. Has no Shell. Two species.
Clio Borealis.   Clio Australis.

3. Cleodora. Two species.

Shell gelatinous, cartilaginous, transparent, in shape of a reversed pyramid or lanceolate truncated, only open at the summit.

Cleodora pyramidata.   Cleodora caudata.

C. pyramidata. The pyramidal Cleodora.

Like a pyramid, triangular, thin, transparent; aperture obliquely truncated.

4. Limacina. One species.

Shell papyraceous, very fragile, planorbis form, sub-carinated, involuted rather obliquely, in such a manner as to be deeply and largely umbilicated on one side, and the spine slightly projecting and pointed on the other; aperture large, entire.

L. helicialis. The Helix-like Limacina.

Thin, fragile, spiral; the volutions united in a discoid form.

5. Cymbulia. The Slipper. One species.

Shell or case cartilaginous, transparent, conical posteriorly where the animal adheres, and prolonged above like a long hollow semi-cylinder, under which the animal can take shelter.

C. Peronii. Peron's Cymbulia.

Shell shaped like a shoe, somewhat gelatinous or cartilaginous, very transparent crystalline, oblong pointed at the vertex, truncated at the base.

6. Pneumodermon. Has no shell. One species.

P. Peronii.

FAMILY II.

PHYLLIDIACEA. Four genera.

1. Phyllidia. Three species.

The animals of this genus are covered with a coriaceous skin, but without a shell.

Phyllidia varicosa.   Phyllidia pustulosa.
P. ocellata.

2. Chitonellus. Two species.

Formerly classed with the Chiton; but as the testaceous

plates of this genus are never joined, the two may be easily distinguished.

Shell elongated, multivalve; alternate pieces generally longitudinal; sides naked.

  Chitonellus striatus.   Chitonellus larvæformis.

C. striatus. The striated Chitonellus.

Striæ radiating from the apex of each valve; margin serrated; base of the last valve obtuse.

C. larvæformis. The Caterpillar Chitonellus.

More or less cylindrical, almost naked; the valves of the shell very small, and almost entirely concealed under the skin; tufts hairy or silky between the parts of the valves near the margin.

3. Chiton. Six species.

This genus was so called from the resemblance of its testaceous covering to a coat of mail. The form of the Chiton is very similar to a well-known insect called the woodlouse, found in decayed timber; it generally adheres to rocks, or lies rolled up like a ball among seaweed and stones. In length it seldom exceeds an inch, except in tropical climates, where they are sometimes three or four inches long. In general there are eight valves, the termination of which is surrounded by a scaly or rough ligament, which enables the animal to expand or contract its shell freely. It presents a great variety of colour; in general it is dark brown, overcast with a shade of green, but some are beautifully variegated with pink, yellow, blue, or red; interior green or whitish.

Shell more or less elongated, consisting of a longitudinal series of eight very symmetrical calcareous pieces, more or less curved, and round at both extremities; summit more or less marked, and when imbricated, always from front to rear.

 Chiton gigas.   Chiton spinosus.
 C. squamosus.   C. fascicularis.
 C. Peruvianus.   C. marginatus.

C. squamosus. The scaly Chiton. Pl. 1, fig. 1.

Depressed, valves large, carinated, well imbricated; the interstices offering well-marked lateral spaces; the border of the mantle regularly scaly.

C. marginatus. The marginated Chiton. Pl. 1, fig. 2.

Valves carinated and projecting over each other; finely shagreened, with a dusky reddish-brown margin.

C. fascicularis. The fasciculated Chiton. Pl. 1, fig. 3.

Valves more narrow, imbricated, without distinct spaces; lateral parts of the skin naked or hairy, but always provided with silky or hairy tufts disposed in pairs between the junctions of the valve.

C. spinosus. The spiny Chiton. Pl. 1, fig. 4.

Shell beset with long, thin, curved, tubular, hairy, blackish spines.

4. Patella. The Limpet or Dishlike Shell. Forty-five species.

The Patella of Linnæus was divided by Lamarck into several distinct genera, and now comprehends only such shells as are of a conical form, with an imperforated summit. The anterior is that part to which the summit inclines, and is always more narrow than the posterior part.

It derives its name from its resemblance to a little dish; the colour and structure are various; some are smooth, others granulated, and many are covered with elevated tuberculated ribs. The exterior is sometimes of a pale fawn colour, and the interior of a bright pink; some have a silvery hue, but the more general colour is bluish white or light brown.

This genus of shells is very numerous in all seas, but chiefly in hot countries, where they are found of a larger size; they generally adhere by their base to rocks, stones, and marine substances, from which it is difficult to detach them.

Shell oval or circular, sub-conic; summit right or more or less recurved anteriorly; the cavity simple, entire, more or less deep; the margin complete and entirely horizontal; a narrow muscular impression.

Patella apicina.	Patella Safiana.
P. granatina.	P. testudinaria.
P. oculus.	P. cochlear.
P. barbara.	P. compressa.
P. plicata.	P. granularis.
P. laciniosa.	P. decaurata.
P. saccharina.	P. Magellanica.
P. angulosa.	P. stellifera.
P. barbata.	P. vulgata.
P. longicosta.	P. mammillaris.
P. spinifera.	P. lineata.
P. aspera.	P. leucopleura.
P. luteola.	P. notata.
P. pyramidata.	P. Tarentina.
P. umbrella.	P. punctata.
P. plumbea.	P. puncturata.
P. cærulea.	P. Javanica.
P. radians.	P. tuberculifera.
P. scutellaris.	P. miniata.
P. viridula.	P. pellucida.
P. pectinata.	P. tricostata.
P. Galathea.	P. Australis.

P. cymbularia.

P. vulgata. The common Patella. Pl. 2, fig. 1.

Conic, summit obtuse and vertical; sometimes ribbed from the vertex to the margin with divergent striæ, sometimes striated without ribs; exterior dark brown or greenish, internal blue or purple radiations.

P. compressa. The compressed or flat-sided Patella. Pl. 2, fig. 2.

Oval, elongated, compressed on the sides, having the

summit sub-anterior, well marked, and curved; exterior fawn colour, interior of a silvery hue.

P. deaurata. The golden red Patella. Pl. 2, fig. 3.

Sub-conic, summit more anterior, with a slight forward inclination; colour yellowish red.

P. cochlear. The spoonlike Patella. Pl. 2, fig. 4.

Depressed, the summit hardly marked, and much more narrow in front than behind; exterior brownish, interior light blue.

P. scutellaris. The buckler Patella. Pl. 2, fig. 5.

Depressed, summit sub-anterior, radiated from the summit to the margin; brown colour, with a yellowish band parallel to the margin.

P. pectinata. The pectinated Patella. Pl. 2, fig. 6.

Oval, summit well marked and anteriorly inclined; ribbed from the summit to the margin, which is slightly convex in the middle.

P. cymbularia. The cymbular Patella. Pl. 2, fig. 7.

Oval, thin, pearly, with a festooned margin; summit nearly marginal; colour white, shaded with very light brown.

FAMILY III.
CALYPTRACEA. Seven genera.

The genera that constitute this family were separated by Lamarck from the Patella of Linnæus.

1. Parmaphora. The Duck's-bill Limpet. Three species.

The characteristic distinctions of this shell were first pointed out by De Blainville.

Shell elongated, very depressed; the summit greatly post-medial, and evidently inclined behind; aperture as large as the shell; the lateral edges straight and parallel, the posterior rounded, the anterior sharp and notched in the middle;

muscular impression large, elongated oval, slightly open in front.

   Parmophora Australis.   Parmophora brevicula.
        P. granulata.

P. Australis. The Australian Parmophorus.

Shell oblong, depressed; vertex slightly recurved; striated concentrically; one margin rounded, and the other truncated.

  2. Emarginula. The Slit Limpet. Four species.

Most of the shells of this genus are small; some are elevated, and others of a widely-depressed conical form.

Shell conical, recurved; summit entire; slit, or more or less hollowed on the anterior side; a muscular impression in form of a horseshoe, open behind and thicker at the beginning.

   Emarginula Blainvillii. Emarginula fissura.
   E. marginata.   E. rubra.

 E. Blainvillii. Blainville's Emarginula.

Shell with the notch or slit in the middle of the back, and not extending to the margin.

E. fissura. The slit Emarginula. Pl. 32, fig. 5.

Oval, compressed, summit well marked, with reticulated striæ and ribs; fissure extending half way from the margin to the summit; exterior light brown, interior white.

E. marginata. The marginated Emarginula.

More compressed than the preceding; summit distinct, anterior margin formed like a gutter.

  3. Fissurella. The Keyhole Limpet. Nineteen species.

The perforation not being perfectly round, but generally ovate oblong, procured for this genus its common name, by which it is easily distinguished.

Shell simple, conical, depressed, recurved; summit perforated a little anterior in an oblong or oval manner, like a keyhole; the exterior surface ribbed longitudinally, slightly striated transversely.

Fissurella picta.	Fissurella radiata.
F. nimbosa.	F. viridula.
F. crassa.	F. hiantula.
F. Græca.	F. pustula.
F. nodosa.	F. fascicularis.
F. Cayennensis.	F. Javanicensis.
F. lilacina.	F. depressa.
F. rosea.	F. Peruviana.
F. Barbadensis.	F. gibberula.
F. minuta.	

F. nimbosa. The scaly-ribbed Fissurella.

Species of which the middle part of the edges of the aperture is hollowed in such a manner that, when placed on a level surface, they touch only at the extremities.

F. rosea. The rosy Fissurella.

Species more depressed, edges bent up lengthwise, forming a kind of canal.

F. Græca. The Greek Fissurella. Pl. 32, fig. 1.

Conical, ovate oblong; striæ cancellated and elevated; sections tuberculated; exterior yellowish brown or clouded, interior white or light blue.

4. Pileopsis. The Caplike Limpet. Four species.

Easily distinguished by its form, which gave rise to the common name.

Shell oblique, sharp pointed; cone bent forward, with a recurved, almost spiral summit, finely striated longitudinally and slightly wrinkled transversely; aperture a round oval; the margin at the base nearly round, more or less regularly crenated and indented, interior with a lengthened, arched, transverse muscular impression.

Pileopsis ungarica.	Pileopsis intorta.
P. mitrula.	P. subrufa.

P. ungarica. The Fool's Cap.

Conical, vertex slightly spiral, pointed, and recurved; exterior pale fawn colour, and the outer margin bordered with a fringed epidermis; interior sometimes of a very bright pink or rose colour.

5. Calyptræa. The Cup and Saucer Limpet. Four species.

This genus of shells is remarkable for having in the interior cavity a transverse funnel or tongue-shaped testaceous appendage, from which originated its common name.

Shell conic, base orbicular; summit vertical and imperforated; cavity deep, having at its interior summit a tongue-like appendage. This appendage is sometimes vertical and sometimes like a horseshoe, having on it a muscular impression of variable form.

Calyptræa extinctorium.   Calyptræa equestris.
C. lævigata.   C. tectum-sinense.

C. extinctorium. The extinguisher Calyptræa.

Species in which the internal appendage is horn-shaped; colour brownish.

C. equestris. The equestrian Calyptræa. Pl. 32, fig. 4.

Species in which the internal appendage is like a horseshoe, open in front.

C. tectum-sinense. The Chinese roof Calyptræa.

Shell formed of separate, transverse, irregular round laminæ of uniform size, attached to each other by the summit on the exterior of each, presenting the appearance of a number of small flat Patellæ piled one on the other; colour yellowish, margin entire, very glossy within.

6. Crepidula. The Slipper Limpet. Six species.

Very similar to the Navicella, but distinguished from it by not having an operculum.

Shell irregular, form very variable, depressed or compressed; spire obliquely inclined to one side; margin entire;

cavity large, divided by a horizontal partition, which gives it the form of a half-decked boat.

Crepidula fornicata.	Crepidula unguiformis.
C. porcellana.	C. dilatata.
C. aculeata.	C. Peruviana.

C. porcellana. The brown-spotted Crepidula. Shell thick, flat, summit not spiral.

C. aculeata. The prickly Crepidula.
Oval, brown, roughly striated, vertex recurved, interior blue or purple.

C. sub-spirata. The sub-spiral Crepidula. Pl. 32, fig. 2.
Species almost round, summit sub-spiral; colour yellowish white, with a bluish tinge towards the summit.

7. Ancylus. The Lake Limpet. Two species.

This is a fresh-water shell, found in the lakes of Europe. Shell thin and brittle, obliquely conical; summit pointed and recurved; margins simple, base oval and smooth.

Ancylus oblongus.   Ancylus fluviatilis.

A. oblongus. The oblong Ancylus.
Aperture elongated, vertex turned to one side, striated concentrically; exterior pale yellowish colour, interior light blue.

A. fluviatilis. The river Ancylus. Pl. 32, fig. 3.
Simple, oval, almost symmetrical; summit pointed, compressed, very distinct; bent back a little to the right, but not marginal; the edges of the aperture entire and effuse.

FAMILY IV.

BULLACEA. Three genera.

1. Acera. Has no shell. One species.

Acera Carnosa.

2. Bullæa. One species.

Formerly classed with the Bulla, but separated from it on

account of the shell being entirely covered by the animal, and never externally visible.

Shell oval, thin, fragile, more or less involuted on one side, rendering the aperture more or less wide.

B. aperta. The open Bullæa. Pl. 17, fig. 5.

Shell interior and very incompletely involuted, without spire or columella; sub-orbicular, white, transparent, faintly striated, and slightly wrinkled; almost entirely open.

3. Bulla. The Bubble. Eleven species.

The great confusion that existed in this genus, as classed by Linnæus, has been elucidated by the division and classification of Lamarck. This genus derived its name from the resemblance which some of the smaller species have to a bubble of water. Its shells are found in almost all parts of the world.

Shell external, oval, involuted; aperture very large, open the whole length of the shell, and generally wider at the base; outer edge sharp and smooth; summit umbilicated.

Bulla lignaria.	Bulla fasciata.
B. ampulla.	B. aplustre.
B. striata.	B. hydatis.
B. naucum.	B. cornea.
B. physis.	B. fragilis.
B. solida.	

B. aplustre. The streamer-like Bulla. Pl. 17, fig. 7.

Species completely involute; the spire very distinct, visible, but not projecting, with a kind of thickening at the anterior part of the columellar edge.

B. lignaria. The woodlike Bulla.

Species sub-involute, no visible spire either within or without, but narrowed towards the top when it is slightly umbilicated; yellowish brown colour, with transverse pale striæ.

B. hydatis. The watery Bulla.

Species more solid, thicker, almost entirely involute;

whorls of the spire slightly visible in an umbilicus projecting interiorly from the summit.

B. naucum. The seanut Bulla.

Species thin; the whorls of the spire visible externally, but without projection, and with a suture as if caniculated without thickening at the anterior part of the columellar edge.

B. fragilis. The fragile Bulla.

Species very thin, rather involute; the whorls of the spire distinct within as without; the suture deep, angular, and cleft in a greater or less part of its length.

FAMILY V.

APLYSIACEA. Two genera.

1. Aplysia. Three species.

This genus may almost be said to have no testaceous covering, as it appears more like the element of a shell.

Aplysia depilans.   Aplysia fasciata.
A. punctata.

A. depilans. The bald Aplysia.

Shell dorsal, semicircular, of a thin yellow cartilaginous substance.

2. Dolabella. Two species.

Closely allied to the Aplysia; it is a singularly formed shell, difficult to describe, as it contains few of the characteristics which distinguish other shells.

Shell rudimentary, entirely flat, sub-spiral, with a summit thick and very callous.

Dolabella Rumphii.   Dolabella fragilis.

D. Rumphii. Rumphius's Dolabella.

Base thick, callous, and sub-spiral; dilated above, thin, and wedge-shaped.

FAMILY VI.

LIMACINEA. Five genera.

1. Onchidium. Has no shell. Two species.

Onchidium Typhæ.   Onchidium Peronii.

2. Parmacella. One species.

Lamarck has given a description of the animal of this genus, but only mentions that the scutcheon contains a shell or solid crustaceous body.

Parmacella Olivieri.

3. Limax. Four species.

The animal belonging to this genus is furnished with a coriaceous shield, wrinkled.

Limax rufus.   Limax cinerus.
L. albus.   L. agrestis.

4. Testacella. One species.

Shell external, very small, ear-shaped; very depressed, summit inclined posteriorly, not spiral; aperture oval, very large; the left edge sharp, a little rolled inward, especially behind.

T. Haliotidea. The Haliotis-shaped Testacella. Pl. 17, fig. 6.

Answering to the above description; very thin, transparent, and yellowish.

5. Vitrina. One species.

Shell proportionally very small, extremely thin, pellucid, almost membranous, oval or sub-globular; spire very short, of which the last whorl is very large; aperture large, semilunar; the edges sharp; the left edge arched, and extending itself interiorly to the summit.

V. pellucida. The pellucid Vitrina. Pl. 17, fig. 3.

Extremely thin, pellucid, and glossy; depressed, spire

very short; aperture large and oval; colour pale yellowish green.

FAMILY VII.

COLIMACEA. Eleven genera.

1. Helix. The Snail. One hundred and seven species.

According to the systematic arrangement of Lamarck, this genus now consists of shells with peculiar characteristic distinctions.

By Linnæus, marine, land, and fresh-water shells were united in this genus, and so confounded that the naturalist would often look in vain for the distinguishing characters which would enable him to class and determine the genus of the object under examination.

Notwithstanding the divisions of Lamarck, its species are numerous; the shells are terrestrial, and found in all parts of the globe; some are rare and beautiful.

The term Helix was given to this genus from the spiral form of the shell.

Shell extremely variable in form, generally globular, sometimes ventricose, conoid, never turriculated; summit constantly obtuse and rounded; aperture generally of a medium size, but sometimes very large or very small, always modified by the turn of the spire; oval, semi-lunar, more wide than long, edges disunited, entering but very little into the formation of the interior; the right lip or margin thickened or reflected.

Helix vesicalis.	Helix mutata.
H. algira.	H. gigantea.
H. pomatia.	H. polyzonalis.
H. aspersa.	H. monozonalis.
H. vermiculata.	H. pulla.
H. alonensis.	H. versicolor.
H. lineolata.	H. Naticoides.
H. picta.	H. Madagascariensis.

H. galactites.
H. hæmastoma.
H. melanotragus.
H. extensa.
H. lucana.
H. globulus.
H. melanostoma.
H. cælatura.
H. microstoma.
H. maculosa.
H. Richardi.
H. Bonplandii.
H. planulata.
H. labrella.
H. ungulina.
H. pellis-serpentis.
H. Senegalensis.
H. unidentata.
H. cepa.
H. heteroclites.
H. discolor.
H. lactea.
H. zonaria.
H. serpentina.
H. Niciensis.
H. variabilis.
H. fruticum.
H. neglecta.
H. cespitum.
H. ericetorum.
H. intersecta.
H. Carthusianella.
H. Carthusiana.
H. diaphana.
H. concolor.
H. velutina.

H. Javanica.
H. Peruviana.
H. simplex.
H. cidaris.
H. citrina.
H. guttata.
H. verticillus.
H. olivetorum.
H. planospira.
H. Barbadensis.
H. sinuata.
H. hippocastanum.
H. bidentalis.
H. argilacea.
H. vittata.
H. alanda.
H. arbustorum.
H. candidissima.
H. nemoralis.
H. hortensis.
H. sylvatica.
H. pisana.
H. splendida.
H. crenulata.
H. planorbula.
H. macularia.
H. maritima.
H. strigata.
H. muralis.
H. rugosa.
H. cornea.
H. linguifera.
H. incarnata.
H. cinctella.
H. cellaria.
H. nitida.

H. obvoluta.	H. plebeium.
H. Cookiana.	H. personata.
H. pileus.	H. hispida.
H. papilla.	H. rotundata.
H. punctifera.	H. apicina.
H. plicatula.	H. striata.
H. planorbella.	H. conspurcata.
H. scabra.	H. conica.
H. cariosa.	H. conoidea.

H. pulchella.

H. algira. The yellow Snail. Pl. 18, fig. 8.
Species shaped like a Planorbis, rough or hairy, more or less largely umbilicated, margin sharp.

H. Naticoides. The Natica-shaped Snail. Pl. 18, fig. 7.
Species ventricose.

H. obvoluta. The small white-lipped Snail. Pl. 18, fig. 9.
Species more or less depressed, umbilicated, Planorbis-shaped, the edges of the aperture thickened, callous, and even toothed.

H. conoides. The cone-shaped Snail. Pl. 18, fig. 4.
Species conoidal; the turns of the spire rounded.

H. pomatia. The edible Snail.
Species sub-globular, not umbilicated; the margin of the aperture thickened; aperture covered with a calcareous lid resembling an operculum.

H. nitida. The pellucid Snail.
Species depressed, more or less largely umbilicated; the edges sharp, but always thin and shining.

H. nemoralis. The grove Snail.
Species imperforated, semi-globular, thin, and sub-pellucid; not umbilicated, with a light inflexion at the place of the junction of the columella with the margin of the aper-

ture; colour various, inner margin white or reddish brown; volutions five, with several dark brown bands.

H. Carthusiana. The Carthusian Snail.

Species sub-depressed, sub-umbilicated, with a sharp edge, thickened within by a roll.

H. arbustorum. The orchard Snail.

Sub-globular, sub-pellucid, sub-umbilicated, five volutions, finely striated longitudinally; mottled with greenish yellow, streaked with deep chestnut, a broad brown band commonly at the edge of the outer lip, and running round through the volutions to the apex.

2. Carocolla. Eighteen species.

All terrestrial shells in this genus, taken from the Linnæan Helix on account of the peculiarity of the shell, which is orbicular, more or less flat on the upper part; the circumference of the shells constantly carinated or sub-carinated; aperture ovate, transverse, contiguous to the axis of the shells; outer lip sub-angular, sometimes toothed within.

Carocolla acutissima.	Carocolla Madagascariensis.
C. albilabris.	C. marginata.
C. angistoma.	C. lychnuchus.
C. labyrinthus.	C. planata.
C. lucerna.	C. planaria.
C. inflata.	C. hispidula.
C. Gualteriana.	C. lapicida.
C. bicolor.	C. albella.
C. Mauritiana.	C. elegans.

C. lapicida. The stone Carocolla. Pl. 19, fig. 1.

Species discoid, very umbilicated; edges thick, but not toothed; beautiful bands.

C. elegans. The elegant Carocolla.

Species with a conical spire a little elevated, the base flat, the aperture square, with sharp edges.

C. labyrinthus. The winding Carocolla.
Species discoid, umbilicated, with the aperture toothed.

3. Anostoma. Two species.

An extraordinary shell, sometimes called the antique lamp from its form.

Shell orbicular, the spire convex and obtuse; aperture round, toothed within, grinning, turned upward to the spire; margin reflected.

    Anostoma depressa.   Anostoma globulosa.

A. depressa. The depressed Anostoma.

Sub-globular, depressed and sub-carinated in its circumference, not umbilicated; aperture round, the margin continued by a callosity, toothed, thickened, and turned towards the back of the shell.

A. globulosa. The globular Anostoma.

Globose, with two small punctures, one on each side of the lip; slightly carinated, smooth, and white; margin reflected.

4. Helicina. Four species.

A terrestrial shell, distinguished from the Helix by its transverse callous columella; depressed and diminished in thickness at the lower part.

Shell sub-globular or conoid, spire low, a little depressed; aperture semi-ovate, modified by the last turn of the spire; the edge of the aperture sharp or a little reflected in a roll, the left edge enlarged at its base in a large callosity, which entirely covers the umbilicus and joins obliquely with the columella, which is twisted and a little projecting; the operculum horny, complete, sometimes calcareous externally.

    Helicina Neritella.   Helicina fasciata.
    H. striata.   H. viridis.

H. Neritella. The Nerite-shaped Helicina. Pl. 19, fig. 4.
Species yellowish white, finely striated, the edge reflected in a roll.

H. striata. The striated Helicina.

Globular, striated, the right edge sharp, but reflected; the umbilical callosity rather thick, the operculum calcareous and solidified by a marginal roll and a vertical crosspiece.

5. Pupa. Twenty-seven species.

These shells are generally very small, some not more than an eighth of an inch in length; chiefly terrestrial.

Shell cylindrical, elongated, or sub-globular, ordinarily ventricose; summit obtuse; the turns of the spire numerous, almost equal; aperture round or oval, with margins almost equal, expanded, reflected; one or two plaits on the columellar edge, and several teeth, varying in number on the right margin.

Pupa mumia.	Pupa zebra.
P. uva.	P. unicarinata.
P. sulcata.	P. maculosa.
P. candida.	P. clavulata.
P. labrosa.	P. ovularis.
P. fusus.	P. Germanica.
P. tridentata.	P. cinerea.
P. fasciolata.	P. tridens.
P. quadridens.	P. avena.
P. polyodon.	P. granum.
P. variabilis.	P. fragilis.
P. frumentum.	P. dolium.
P. secalis.	P. umbilicata.

P. muscorum.

P. Lyonetiana. Lyonet's Pupa. Pl. 18, fig. 5.

Species cylindrical, obtuse, aperture compressed and distorted by the last whorl in its adult state making suddenly a gibbous inflection to the left.

P. muscorum. The moss Pupa.

Species very small, oval or more or less spherical, obtuse, light brownish colour; aperture large, with one tooth; volutions convex; outer lip white and reflected.

P. mumia. The double-toothed Pupa. Pl. 19, fig. 2.

Species cylindrical, obtuse at both ends, aperture semi-ovate, with two teeth.

6. Clausilia. Twelve species.

Remarkable for having the termination of the lower whorl quite detached from the base of the shell.

Shell cylindrical, elongated, a little ventricose in the middle, generally fusiform, summit obtuse, the last turn smaller than the preceding; aperture small, irregular, oval; at least one plait, posterior to the columella, increasing with age so as to be separated, and forming at the posterior angle of the aperture a rounded sinus.

Clausilia torticollis.	Clausilia teres.
C. truncatula.	C. denticulata.
C. retusa.	C. collaris.
C. costulata.	C. papillaris.
C. corrugata.	C. plicatula.
C. inflata.	C. rugosa.

C. lævis. The smooth Clausilia. Pl. 19, fig. 3.
A regular type of this genus.

C. papillaris. The pimpled Clausilia.
Pellucid, finely striped longitudinally, the margins of the volutions papillose; aperture with two plaits; brownish colour.

7. Bulimus. Thirty-four species.

The shells of this beautiful genus are all terrestrial, and differ from the Helix and Bulla of Linnæus in never being of an orbicular shape. The animals inhabiting them are said to be oviparous, and have eggs nearly as large as those of a pigeon.

Shell oval, oblong, sometimes sub-turriculated; the summit of the spire obtuse, and the last turn much greater than all the others taken together; aperture oblong oval, the edge disunited; the right reflected outward in adults; the columella smooth, with an inflection in the middle, at the point of junction of the columella with the mouth of the aperture which it forms.

Bulimus ovatus.	Bulimus Richii.
B. hæmastomus.	B. inversus.
B. gallina sultana.	B. citrinus.
B. zigzag.	B. sultanus.
B. undatus.	B. Pythogaster.
B. ovoideus.	B. Mexicanus.
B. interruptus.	B. multifasciatus.
B. Peruvianus.	B. Bengalensis.
B. Favannii.	B. Caribæorum.
B. Kambeul.	B. octonus.
B. calcareus.	B. terebraster.
B. decollatus.	B. articulatus.
B. Lyonetianus.	B. acutus.
B. inflatus.	B. ventricosus.
B. radiatus.	B. montanus.
B. fragilis.	B. hordeaceus.
B. Guadaloupensis.	B. lubricus.

B. montanus. The mountain Bulimus.

Ovate oblong, umbilicated, slightly striated longitudinally, with several convex volutions; aperture semi-oval; brownish colour; outer lip white and reflected.

B. hæmastomus. The rose-lipped Bulimus.
Species oval or of ordinary form.

B. ventricosus. The ventricose Bulimus.
Species ventricose, from which circumstance it derived its name.

B. radiatus. The radiated Bulimus. Pl. 19, fig. 7.
Species turriculated.

B. citrinus. The citron Bulimus.
Species sinistral.

B. multifasciatus. The many-banded Bulimus.
Species slightly umbilicated.

8. Achatina. Twenty species.

This likewise is an elegant genus of shells, classed by Linnæus with the Bulla. They are the largest land-shells known, and greatly resemble the Bulimus, but never have their lips reflected or thickened. Sometimes the last whorl is compressed and attenuated at the base, and sometimes ventricose and not compressed.

Shell in form very variable, but generally sub-turriculated, ventricose, striated longitudinally; the summit papillose; aperture a little variable, but never thickened or reflected; the right edge always acute, the columellar margin rather strongly hollowed, entirely formed by the columella, of which the anterior extremity is constantly open and truncated.

Achatina perdix.	Achatina immaculata.
A. zebra.	A. purpurea.
A. acuta.	A. ustulata.
A. bicarinata.	A. vexillum.
A. Mauritiana.	A. Virginea.
A. castanea.	A. Priamus.
A. glans.	A. fulminea.
A. Peruviana.	A. columnaria.
A. albo-lineata.	A. folliculus.
A. fusco-lineata.	A. acicula.

A. Virginea. The Virginian Achatina.

Smooth, conoid, with aperture almost round; very short, grayish white, with red and black transverse bands; columella rose-coloured, with one plait; volutions ventricose; inside of the lips bluish; a transverse callosity in the interior.

A. zebra. The zebra Achatina. Pl. 18, fig. 1.

Species thin, oval, sub-ventricose, spire prominent, striped like a zebra.

A. glans. The acorn Achatina. Pl. 18, fig. 2.

Species sub-turriculated, of which the last whorl is attenuated anteriorly.

P

A. columnaris. The columnar Achatina. Pl. 18, fig. 3. Species evidently turriculated.

9. Succinea. Three species.

A terrestrial shell, though the animal that inhabits it is almost amphibious; it greatly resembles the Bulimus, but is easily distinguished by never having the lip reflected or thickened.

Shell very thin, translucid, ovate-oblong, with a conical-pointed spire formed of a small number of whorls; aperture very large, oval, oblique; the edges disunited; the right always acute, the left acute and arched, formed by the columella.

Succinea cucullata.   Succinea amphibia.
S. oblonga.

S. amphibia. The amphibious Succinea. Pl. 24, fig. 4.
Species elongated, very thin and pellucid; spire short; aperture expanding; amber colour.

10. Auricula. Fourteen species.

This genus was so called from the resemblance which the aperture bears to the shape of an ear; many of the species are named from their resemblance to the ears of particular quadrupeds. It is a land-shell, found chiefly in the East and West India Islands.

Shell thick, solid, more or less smooth, oval, oblong, spire short and obtuse; aperture entire, oblong, enlarged, ear-shaped, much contracted behind; edges disunited; right lip sometimes thick and outwardly reflected; the left or columella with one or more teeth or thick callous plaits.

Auricula Midæ.	Auricula scarabæus.
A. Judæ.	A. bovina.
A. Sileni.	A. caprella.
A. leporis	A. myosotis.
A. felis.	A. minima.
A. Dombeiana.	A. nitens.
A. coniformis.	A. monile.

A. Judæa. Judas's Ear. Pl. 19, fig. 6.

Species thick, oblong, conical, with minute decussated striæ and granulations; light brown; two plaits on the columella; right outwardly reflected.

A. scarabæus. The Beetle's Ear.

Species of which the columella has three plaits, and the whole internal side of the right edge denticulated.

A. myosotis. The dwarf Auricula.

Species minute, with two plaits on the columella, and one tooth behind.

A. Sileni. Silenus's Ear.

Species very small, without plaits or teeth.

11. Cyclostoma. Twenty-eight species.

A terrestrial shell, varying considerably in form, but distinguished by a round aperture, reflected lip, and horny operculum.

Shell more or less elevated, volutions rounded, summit papillose; aperture round, the edges united circularly and reflected; the left having its origin very detached from the spire.

Operculum calcareous, complete, not spiral; summit subcentral.

Cyclostoma planorbula.	Cyclostoma fasciata.
C. volvulus.	C. mumia.
C. carinata.	C. quaternata.
C. sulcata.	C. ferruginea.
C. unicarinata.	C. decussata.
C. tricarinata.	C. lineolata.
C. obsoleta.	C. mamillaris.
C. rugosa.	C. ligata.
C. labeo.	C. lincinella.
C. interrupta.	C. orbella.
C. ambigua.	C. fimbriata.
C. semilabris.	C. multilabris.
C. flavula.	C. elegans.
C. patulum.	C. truncatulum.

C. elegans. The elegant Cyclostoma. Pl. 19, fig. 5.
Species with spire slightly elevated, ovate, conical, umbilicated; volutions convex; finely striated transversely.

C. fasciata. The banded Cyclostoma.
Species with spire very elevated.

C. Planorbula. The Planorbis-shaped Cyclostoma.
Species with spire very depressed.

FAMILY VIII.
LYMNÆCEA. Three genera.

1. Planorbis. Twelve species.

Taken from the Helix of Linnæus to distinguish the aquatic from the terrestrial shells. This genus is found in fresh water, and has no operculum.

Shell thin, often sinistral, discoid, or involuted almost in the same vertical plane; the spire not projecting and entirely lateral, so that the shell is hollowed or depressed on each side; aperture small, transverse, with edges sharp, not reflected, disunited by the last whorl of the spire which modifies it; sometimes carinated.

Planorbis cornu-arietis.	Planorbis vortex.
P. corneus.	P. deformis.
P. carinatus.	P. contortus.
P. lutescens.	P. hispidus.
P. orientalis.	P. nitidus.
P. spirorbis.	P. imbricatus.

P. carinatus. The keeled Planorbis.
Species with a keel; depressed, upper side concave.

P. corneus. The horny Planorbis. Pl. 20, fig. 4.
Species without a keel.

2. Physa. Four species.

This genus is generally heterostrophe (that is, with whorls turned to the left hand); found in fresh water; it greatly resembles the Lymnæa, but has not a widened aperture.

Shell often sinistral, oval, oblong, or globular, perfectly smooth; aperture oval, contracted posteriorly; the right edge sharp, advanced above the plane of the left edge; columella twisting obliquely, and enlarging to join itself to the anterior part of the columellar margin.

Physa castanea.   Physa hypnorum.
P. fontinalis.   P. subopaca.

P. fontinalis. The fountain Physa. Pl. 20, fig. 2.

Volutions reversed, oval, ventricose, pellucid, horn-coloured; spire short and acute.

3. Lymnæa. Eleven species.

Shell aquatic, oval, turreted or conical, thin, smooth, spire pointed; aperture oval, entire; edges disunited, the left with a very oblique plait at the point of junction of the columella with the rest of the margin.

Lymnæa stagnalis.   Lymnæa auricularia.
L. palustris.   L. ovata.
L. Virginiana.   L. peregra.
L. luteola.   L. intermedia.
L. acuminata.   L. leucostoma.
L. minuta.

L. stagnalis. The pond Lymnæa. Pl. 20, fig. 1.

Ovate, ventricose; spire subulate and very acute; aperture large and ovate; horn coloured.

L. leucostoma. The shining Lymnæa.

Species sub-turreted, with the right edge thickened.

FAMILY IX.

MELANIDES. Three genera.

1. Melania. Sixteen species.

Likewise taken from the Helix of Linnæus.

Shell fluviatile, covered with epidermis, oval, oblong; spire slightly pointed, more or less turreted; the margin of the whorls often surmounted by spires; aperture oval, entire; columella smooth and arched; closed by a thin, horny, complete operculum.

Melania asperata.	Melania decollata.
M. truncata.	M. amarula.
M. coarctata.	M. thiarella.
M. punctata.	M. spinulosa.
M. corrugata.	M. granifera.
M. subulata.	M. carinifera.
M. lævigata.	M. truncatula.
M. clavus.	M. fasciolata.

M. amarula. The crowned Melania. Pl. 20, fig. 3.

Covered with a black epidermis, under which the colour is deep chestnut; ovate oblong, with the whorls transversely keeled and coronated with triangular tubercles, from which emanate ciliated spines.

2. Melanopsis. Three species.

The shells of this genus are fluviatile, and distinguished from the Melania by having the upper part of the columella callous.

Shell oval or slightly sub-turriculated; aperture oval, without trace of tube, but hollowed anteriorly, without a posterior sinus; the columellar edge callous and rather deeply excavated; operculum horny, sub-spiral, rather complete.

Melanopsis Buccinoides. Melanopsis costata.
M. lævigata.

M. Buccinoides. The Buccinum-shaped Melanopsis. Pl. 20, fig. 6.

Species turriculated; colour bluish white, clouded with purple; spiral whorls dentated.

M. costata. The ribbed Melanopsis.
Species sub-turriculated and ribbed.

M. lævigata. The polished Melanopsis.
Species ovate, smooth, chestnut colour.

3. Pirena. Four species.

This shell resembles the Melania, but is easily distinguished by having a sinus at the base and another at the summit.

Shell turreted, aperture oblong, closed by a horny operculum; right lip sharp, with a distinct sinus at the base and another at the summit; base of the columella inclined towards the right.

Pirena terebralis.   Pirena aurita.
P. spinosa.   P. granulosa.

P. terebralis. The wimble Pirena.
Subulate, longitudinally striated, covered with a dark-brown epidermis; aperture white, outer lip expanded.

FAMILY X.

PERISTOMIDES. Three genera.

1. Valvata. One species.

This genus contains shells found in fresh water.

Shell sub-discoid or conoid, umbilicated, spiral whorls rounded; summit papillose; aperture round, not modified by the last whorl; the edges completely united, sharp; operculum complete, horny, and orbicular.

V. piscinalis. The Pond Valvata. Pl. 20, fig. 5.
Small, globular, conoid, deeply umbilicated; summit obtuse; wrinkled longitudinally, covered with a yellowish epidermis.

2. Paludina. Seven species.

Generally inhabits fresh water, though some have been found where it is quite saline.

Shell conoid, covered with epidermis, spiral whorls rounded; rather longer than broad, edges united, always sharp; the commencement of the left edge immediately attached to the last whorl of the spire; operculum horny, complete, or marginal, not spiral, with concentric elements.

Paludina vivipara.　　Paludina unicolor.
P. achatina.　　　　　P. impura.
P. Bengalensis.　　　 P. muriatica.
　　　　　　P. viridis.

P. vivipara. The viviparous Paludina. Pl. 21, fig. 1.

Thin, ovate, ventricose, wrinkled longitudinally; body with three brown bands; covered with a greenish epidermis; aperture almost round.

3. Ampullaria. Eleven species.

This genus is evidently intermediary to the Paludina and the Natica. Its species are probably all fluviatile; some attain a great size.

Shell thin, globular, ventricose; umbilicus small, forming a compressed funnel-shaped aperture, without interior callosity; spire very short, the last whorl much larger than all the others together; aperture ovate, longer than broad, with margins united; right margin smooth and sharp; columellar lip thickened, projecting, and reflected over the umbilicus; operculum horny, rarely calcareous, thin, oval, not spiral, with concentric elements; summit sub-marginal, inferior, passing obliquely by the right edge of the aperture, but attached to the left.

Ampullaria Guyanensis.　　Ampullaria Guinaica.
A. rugosa.　　　　　　　　A. virens.
A. fasciata.　　　　　　　 A. carinata.
A. canaliculata.　　　　　A. avellana.
A. effusa.　　　　　　　　 A. intorta.
　　　　　　A. fragilis.

A. Guyanensis. The Guiana Ampullaria.

Globular, thick, with unequal longitudinal striæ; covered with brown epidermis; inside golden colour.

A. rugosa. The rough Ampullaria. Pl. 21, fig. 3.
Species dextral.

A. Guinaica. The Guinea Ampullaria.
Species sinistral.

A. carinata. The carinated Ampullaria.

Species sinistral, with a very large umbilicus, spirally carinated.

FAMILY XI.

NERITACEA. Five genera.

1. Neritina. Twenty-one species.

Formerly classed with the Nerita, but separated from it because the Nerita is a marine shell, and those of this genus are fluviatile.

They are generally thin, smooth, or very finely striated; the right side of the aperture is not crenulated or dentated, and the animal dissolves the interior of the spire.

Shell thin, ovate, not umbilicated; aperture semilunar; inner lip reflected on the columella, and sometimes crenated; outer lip without teeth internally; operculum with a lateral tooth.

Neritina perversa.	Neritina auriculata.
N. pulligera.	N. Domingensis.
N. dubia.	N. fasciata.
N. zebra.	N. lineolata.
N. zigzag.	N. semi-conica.
N. gagates.	N. strigilata.
N. lugubris.	N. meleagris.
N. corona.	N. Virginea.
N. brevi-spina.	N. fluviatilis.
N. crepidularia.	N. viridis.

N. Bætica.

N. fluviatilis. The fresh-water Neritina.

Shell very small, oval; back convex, smooth, white, with black or brown spots; spire inclined, lateral lip slightly denticulated; right edge sharp, operculum very oblique.

N. zebra. The zebra or striped Neritina. Pl. 21, fig. 2.

Same as N. fluviatilis, but striped instead of spotted.

N. corona. The crown Neritina. Pl. 21, fig. 4.

Species provided with long spines, and with the columellar edge denticulated.

N. auriculata. The eared Neritina.

Species with the columellar edge denticulated; the two extremities of the right edge extending beyond the aperture, and forming with the callosity, which is reflected over the columella, a kind or ear, produced by the tentacular lobe of the animal.

N. perversa. The perverse Neritina.

Species shaped like a Calyptræa, with the superior summit vertical, spiral; the last whorl forming all the base of the shell.

2. Navicella. Three species.

A fresh-water shell, closely allied to the Neritina; it generally has the appearance of porcelain.

Shell ovate oblong, covered with epidermis, shaped like a Patella, summit not spiral, but straight, turned quite to the base, and concave beneath; no columella; the columellar edge replaced by a kind of sharp partition, which covers part of the aperture, with a sinus at its left extremity; muscular impression shaped like a horseshoe, open in front and interrupted behind; thin, calcareous operculum, with a subulate, lateral tooth adhering to the posterior margin; the other edges sharp.

Navicella elliptica.   Navicella lineata.
N. tessellata.

N. elliptica. The oval Navicella.

Shell covered with olive epidermis, under which it is smooth, shining, spotted and streaked with purple, blue, or brown; spire curved, prominent, extending beyond the margin.

3. Nerita. The Hoof Shell. Seventeen species.

A marine shell, never spined, but variously striated. Some species of this genus are very beautiful; they are frequently worn as ornaments by the Indians.

Shell solid, thick, more or less globular, flat beneath, spire but little, if at all, projecting, not umbilicated; aperture large, semilunar, very entire; the external margin very much hollowed; the internal or columellar straight, sharp, and shaped like a partition, often dentated; operculum horny or calcareous, sub-spiral; the summit entirely marginal at its extremity, implanted by teeth more or less marked, and sunk in the columellar margin, on which it seems articulated.

Nerita exuvia.	Nerita chamæleon.
N. textilis.	N. versicolor.
N. undata.	N. Ascensionis.
N. peloronta.	N. Malaccensis.
N. chlorostoma.	N. lineata.
N. atrata.	N. scabricosta.
N. polita.	N. plicata.
N. albicilla.	N. tessellata.

N. signata.

N. peloronta. The bleeding-tooth Nerita. Pl. 21, fig. 5.

Thick, transversely sulcated; inner lip with two crenulations, with a bloody mark at their base; under lip with two notches near its internal upper edge; colour yellowish, tinged with red, with variously coloured bands.

N. exuvia. The exuvia Nerita.

Species with the inner lip toothed and tuberculated.

N. polita. The smooth Nerita.

Species with both lips toothed; beautifully distinguished by having three or four bright crimson bands, on a dark mottled ground, running in a parallel direction with the convolutions of the shell. A favourite Indian ornament.

4. Natica. Thirty-one species.

A marine shell, formerly classed with the Nerita, but distinguished by being without teeth, and having an umbilicus modified by the callosity.

Shell smooth, rather thin, and not covered with epidermis; the spire evident, though low, umbilicated; the columellar edge not toothed, more or less callous, modifying the umbilicus; the right edge thin and not toothed interiorly; operculum calcareous or horny and smooth, semispiral, with concentric ribs fitting into a slight groove on the columella.

Natica glaucina.	Natica melanostoma.
N. albumen.	N. aurantia.
N. mamillaris.	N. conica.
N. mamilla.	N. plumbea.
N. ampullaria.	N. lineata.
N. canrena.	N. fulminea.
N. cruentata.	N. maculosa.
N. millepunctata.	N. vittata.
N. vitellus.	N. castanea.
N. helvacea.	N. Marochiensis.
N. collaria.	N. arachnoidea.
N. monilifera.	N. zebra.
N. labrella.	N. zonaria.
N. rufa.	N. Chinensis.
N. uni-fasciata.	N. Javanica.

N. cancellata.

N. canrena. The Canrena Natica.

Sub-globular, smooth, umbilicus deep, bordered anteriorly by a kind of callous column; spire a little prominent; exterior fawn coloured, with bands and rays of reddish brown; interior white; operculum calcareous.

N. castanea. The chestnut Natica. Pl. 21, fig. 6.

Species with the umbilicus uncovered, and the operculum horny.

N. mamilla. The nipple Natica.

Species with the umbilicus entirely covered over by a large callosity; the spire papillose, and the operculum horny.

5. Janthina. Two species.

Formerly classed with the Helix, which it somewhat resembles in form, but properly separated, as it differs in every other respect.

It is a singular marine shell, often found in great numbers floating on the surface of the sea, suspended by a vesicular appendage, which stains the hand of a purple colour.

Shell sub-globular, ventricose, extremely thin and fragile; transparent, of a beautiful violet colour; the spire low, lateral, pointed, with sub-carinated whorls; aperture large, sub-angular, greatly modified by the last whorl of the spire; edges disunited, the left entirely formed by the columella, which is straight and continued beyond the base, the right edge sharp, often with a sinus in the middle.

Janthina communis.   Janthina exigua.

J. communis. The common Janthina. Pl. 18, fig. 6.

Very fragile, aperture triangular, with a small notch on the margin of the outer lip; beautiful violet colour.

FAMILY XII.

MACROSTOMIDES. Four genera.

1. Sigaretus. Four species.

Distinguished from the Natica by the great width of the aperture, and its short spiral columella.

Shell oval, more or less thick, very depressed, spiral short, little elevated, lateral; aperture very extended, entire, the left edge reflected and sharp; two lateral muscular impressions very disunited.

Sigaretus Haliotoideus.   Sigaretus lævigatus.
S. convexus.   S. cancellatus.

S. convexus. The convex Sigaretus. Pl. 22, fig. 2.

Very thin, smooth, back convex, spire white, rather prominent; aperture very expanded; umbilicus rather deep; yellow, with a reddish tinge, transversely striated.

S. Haliotoideus. The Haliotis-shaped Sigaretus.

Species thick, solid, depressed; spire flattish, aperture exposing the whole of the interior.

2. Stomatella. Five species.

To be easily distinguished from the Stomatia by not having a transversal rib.

Shell very depressed, orbicular or oblong; imperforate; interior pearly; aperture very large, oval, longer than wide; the right edge effuse, dilated, and open; summit pointed and incurved.

Stomatella imbricata.   Stomatella sulcifera.
S. rubra.   S. auricula.
S. planulata.

S. imbricata. The imbricated Stomatella. Pl. 22, fig. 1.

Sub-orbicular, convex, sub-depressed, rough, covered with imbricated scales; colour grayish brown.

S. auricula. The ear-shaped Stomatella.

Species oval, elongated.

3. Stomatia. Two species.

Bearing a very great resemblance to the Haliotis, but is never perforated.

Shell ear-shaped, imperforate; oblong, spire elevated and recurved to one side; aperture entire, oblong; interior pearly; tuberculated, and with a transverse sub-carinated rib.

S. phymotis. The tumoured Stomatia. Pl. 22, fig. 6.

Elongated oval, striated, tuberculated; spire small, contorted; lip thin and sharp, colour white, interior pearly.

4. Haliotis. The Ear Shell. Fifteen species.

This genus is very beautiful, and derived its common name from its resemblance to the human ear. The exterior is generally tuberculated and loaded with marine substances, which gives it a rough and uncouth appearance, but the interior forms a splendid contrast by its natural iridescence. Each shell is furnished with a row of orifices near the margin, varying in number from eight upward; of these from three to seven are generally open, and the others close. These holes are made by the animal as it increases the size of the shell, to admit the passage of a short syphon.

They are found adhering to rocks like the Patella, and are detached with great difficulty.

Shell ear-shaped, pearly, recurving, very depressed, more or less oval, with spire very small, very low, almost posterior and lateral; aperture as large as the shell, with margins continued; the right thin and sharp, the left flat, enlarged, and sharp; a series of holes, complete or incomplete, parallel to the left margin; one large oval muscular impression.

Haliotis Midæ.	Haliotis asinina.
H. iris.	H. glabra.
H. tubifera.	H. lamellosa.
H. excavata.	H. unilateralis.
H. Australis.	H. rugosa.
H. tuberculata.	H. canaliculata.
H. striata.	H. tricostalis.

H. dubia.

H. asinina. The asinine Haliotis.

Internal margin very broad, inside pearly, smooth, shining, iridesent, reflecting green, pink, and orange; back clouded with brown and green; striated longitudinally.

H. costata. The ribbed Haliotis. Pl. 22, fig. 4, interior. Pl. 32, fig. 6, exterior.

Species with disk rounded anteriorly.

H. canaliculata. The channelled Haliotis.

Species with disk elevated by a large parallel rib, hollowed interiorly, and with the anterior margin more or less irregular.

H. tuberculata. The tuberculated Haliotis.

Aperture open the whole length of the shell; outer lip irregular, exterior reddish brown, striated longitudinally and wrinkled transversely, with a few raised tubercles; interior pearly, reflecting the most beautiful shades of pink, blue, green, and yellow.

FAMILY XIII.
PLICACEA. Two genera.

1. Tornatella. Six species.

Shell thick, oval, convolute, the spire very short; the last whorl much larger than all the others united; the external thin, sharp, dentated interiorly; one or two large plaits on the columella, of which one serves to separate the two parts of the foot.

Tornatella flammea.	Tornatella auricula.
T. solidula.	T. nitidula.
T. fasciata.	T. pedipes.

T. fasciata. The banded Tornatella.

Spire produced, apex acute, aperture straightened, with one plait on the columella; finely striated transversely, with two white transverse bands; colour purplish red.

T. coniformis. The cone-shaped Tornatella. Pl. 22, fig. 3.

Species like a cone; the spire entirely flat.

2. Pyramidella. Five species.

Shell smooth, not covered with epidermis, conical, elongated or sub-turriculated; aperture semi-oval, entire; the outer lip sharp, dentated interiorly, plaited, enlarged over the umbilicus, which it leaves more or less exposed.

Pyramidella terebellum.   Pyramidella plicata.
P. dolabrata.   P. corrugata.
P. maculosa.

P. dolabrata. The dentated Pyramidella. Pl. 22, fig. 5.,
Answers to the above description; when placed on its base, it falls on one side.

P. terebellum. The wimble Pyramidella.
Smooth, glossy, white, with reddish-brown bands; columella recurved; inside of the lip smooth.

FAMILY XIV.

Scalarides. Three genera.

1. Vermetus. One species.

Resembling in appearance the shell of a Serpula; but the organization of the animal caused this to be made a distinct genus.

Its shells are usually found grouped together or intertwined with each other, and are very remarkable for being attached to marine bodies by the attenuated and pointed extremity of the spire.

Shell conical, tubular, thin, involute spirally, more or less close, with whorls almost completely disunited; free or adherent by intertwining; aperture straight, circular, with edges sharp and complete; several partitions not perforated towards the summit; operculum horny and complete.

V. lumbricales. The wormlike Vermetus. Pl. 23, fig. 3.
A flexuous shell, with a spiral, acute tip, very much resembling a corkscrew; colour reddish brown, sometimes clouded with a darker shade.

2. Scalaria. Seven species.

A marine shell, with a circular aperture like the Cyclostoma, but easily distinguished by its turreted form; longitudinal, elevated ribs, never connected together, rather oblique, and sharp; the shape of the shell is elegant, being a spiral cone, formed by gibbous whorls, unconnected by a columella, gradually increasing from the apex to the base. The colour is generally yellowish or brownish white. When perfect and of good size, they are of great value and highly prized.

Shell sub-turreted, the whorls of the spire more or less pressed and garnished with interrupted longitudinal ribs, formed by the successive preservation of the reflected margin of the aperture, which is small, perfectly round, with edges united, thickened, and outwardly reflected; operculum horny and thin.

Scalaria pretiosa.	Scalaria varicosa.
S. lamellosa.	S. communis.
S. coronata.	S. Australis.
S. raricosta.	

S. pretiosa. The precious Scalaria, more commonly called the Wentle Trap, or Winding Staircase. Pl. 23, fig. 1.

This shell has its spiral whorls separate, and appears like an attenuated tube evolved round a cone; spire detached, with a deep umbilicus; volutions connected by longitudinal ribs; body extremely ventricose; colour cream yellow.

S. communis. The common Scalaria, or false Wentle Trap.

More taper and elongated than the S. pretiosa. It has no umbilicus, and the whorls are closely united.

3. Delphinula. Three species.

A marine shell, which, like the Scalaria, has a round aperture, but its solidity and pearly substance distinguishes it from the Cyclostoma, which is terrestrial.

Shell thick, pearly in the interior, sub-discoid or conical; the spiral whorls sometimes detached, rounded, spiny, with a large umbilicus; aperture round or multrigonal, not modified; edges perfectly united with a small spire, tuberculated exteriorly.

Delphinula laciniata. Delphinula distorta.
D. turbinopsis.

D. laciniata. The fringed Delphinula. Pl. 23, fig. 5.

Shell depressed, umbilicus large, surrounded by large vaulted scales in spiral rows; strong waved spiral striæ; colour reddish purple, variegated with white.

FAMILY XV.

Turbinacea. Seven genera.

1. Solarium. Seven species.

Some shells of this genus are highly valued for their beauty and rarity.

Shell orbicular, involuted almost in the same plane; Planorbis-shaped; the spire of the right side very depressed; umbilicus large and conical, with edges denticulated or not at the entrance; aperture not modified by the last whorl of the spire, which is entirely flat; no columella.

Solarium perspectivum.	Solarium stramineum.
S. granulatum.	S. hybridum.
S. lævigatum.	S. variegatum.
S. luteum.	

S. perspectivum. The perspective Solarium. Pl. 23, fig. 4.

Species very carinated in their circumference; the aperture square; umbilicus large and crenated; colour yellowish, with brown and white bands on the sutures of the volutions.

S. variegatum. The variegated Solarium.

Species sub-carinated, aperture sub-orbicular.

2. Trochus. The Top Shell. Sixty-nine species.

This genus derived its name from its resemblance to a top.

The shells are marine, found in almost all parts of the world; some are smooth, but the greater number are covered with knobs, spines, tuberculations, or undulations.

The long spines on the margin of the T. solaris are placed at regular distances, and resemble the rays of the sun. Many, when decorticated, look like mother-of-pearl; others have a splendid metallic lustre. The T. agglutinans possesses the faculty of covering itself with extraneous substances, such as stones, corals, fragments of shells, &c. Of this species there are two kinds, which, though conchologically known only by one name, are familiarly known by two; the Conchologist and the Mineralogist; the former so called from being loaded with shells, and the latter with stones, &c. Sometimes the Conchologist is loaded with corals only, and then is called the Zoologist.

Shell thick, generally pearly, shaped like a top, spire sometimes depressed, sometimes elevated and pointed at the summit, sharp or carinated at its circumference, umbilicated or not; aperture depressed, angular or sub-angular, sometimes heart-shaped, with edges disunited; the right sharp; the columella arched, twisted, and often projecting forward; operculum horny, thin, with numerous spiral whorls, narrow, and increasing a little from the centre to the circumference.

Trochus imperialis.	Trochus asperatus.
T. longispina.	T. rhodostomus.
T. solaris.	T. spinulosus.
T. Indicus.	T. costulatus.
T. radians.	T. inermis.
T. pileus.	T. agglutinans.
T. calyptræformis.	T. cælatus.
T. fimbriatus.	T. tuber.
T. brevispina.	T. magus.
T. rotularius.	T. merula.
T. stella.	T. argyrostomus.
T. stellaris.	T. Cookii.
T. niloticus.	T. conuloides.
T. pyramidalis.	T. conulus.
T. noduliferus.	T. jujubinus.
T. cærulescens.	T. Javanicus.
T. obeliscus.	T. annulatus.
T. virgatus.	T. doliarius.

T. maculatus.	T. granulatus.
T. granosus.	T. granatum.
T. squarrosus.	T. moniliferus.
T. incrassatus.	T. iris.
T. flammulatus.	T. ornatus.
T. elatus.	T. bicingulatus.
T. marmoratus.	T. calliferus.
T. Mauritianus.	T. umbilicaris.
T. imbricatus.	T. undatus.
T. triserialis.	T. Pharaonis.
T. crenulatus.	T. sagittiferus.
T. asperulus.	T. carneolus.
T. acutus.	T. cinerarius.
T. concavus.	T. excavatus.
T. lineatus.	T. nanus.
T. zizyphinus.	T. pyramidatus.

T. erythroleucos.

T. imperialis. The imperial Trochus. Pl. 23, fig. 6.

Species umbilicated, spire very depressed, sharp and radiated at their circumference by the preservation of an angular canal from the middle of the right margin. This species is rare and beautiful, found in New-Zealand.

T. zizyphinus. The livid Trochus.

Species with strong transverse striæ; colour livid, with undulated streaks of red or brownish carnation.

T. agglutinans. The agglutinating or Carrier Trochus.

Species umbilicated, with spire very depressed; the base much enlarged, and as if excavated by the large projection of the angle of the right edge, which advances much beyond the rounded columellar edge; generally covered with shells, stones, or coral.

T. niloticus. The large marble Trochus.

Species not umbilicated, conical, with base flat and circular; the columella twisted; the aperture very angular.

T. obeliscus. The obelisk Trochus.

Species not umbilicated, conic, elevated, flat and circular base; the termination of the columella strongly twisted, but passing down by the margin, appearing sloped by the advance of an internal longitudinal plait.

T. iris. The iris Trochus.

Species not umbilicated, conic, base oblique; aperture large, slightly angular; the columella twisted, and forming a kind of tooth at its termination.

T. granulatus. The granulated Trochus.

Conic, imperforate at the base, spirally granulated and not marginated at the edges of the volutions; body swelling out; spire tapering abruptly; apex acute, flesh-coloured.

T. umbilicaris. The umbilicated Trochus.

Shell conico-convex, rather flat, rounded at the top; apex depressed, volutions sub-marginate; striated spirally; aperture compressed and angular; umbilicus large, extending to the apex; colour whitish.

3. Monodonta. Twenty-three species.

This genus occupies an intermediate space between the Trochus and the Turbo; distinguished from the former by the aperture being more round and slightly depressed, and from the latter by the toothlike projecting angle which the truncated columella occasions at the base of the aperture.

Shell ovate or conoid, aperture round and entire, with an operculum; outer lip disunited from the body at the top; columella arched and truncated at the base.

Monodonta bicolor.	Monodonta tectum.
M. pagodus.	M. labio.
M. tectum Persicum.	M. Australis.
M. papillosa.	M. canalifera.
M. coronaria.	M. viridis.
M. Egyptiaca.	M. fragarioides.
M. carchedonius.	M. constricta.

M. modulus.	M. tricarinata.
M. articulata.	M. canaliculata.
M. lugubris.	M. Seminigra.
M. punctulata.	M. rosea.

M. lineata.

M. coronaria. The crowned Monodonta.

Species in which the columella greatly projects, and the spire is entirely flat; covered with numerous small tubercles; colour white; the columella tinged with red.

M. labio. The double-lipped Monodonta. Pl. 23, fig. 2.

Species sub-globular, umbilicated, spiral whorls rounded; the columella terminated by a tooth.

M. fragarioides. The strawberry-shaped Monodonta.

Species more or less globular, of which the columella, almost straight, offers but a little obstacle to its junction with the margin.

4. Turbo. The Turban Shell. Thirty-four species.

Distinguished from the Monodonta by never having the columella truncated at the base; and from the Trochus by being solid, with the whorls constantly convex and never flattened. Like the Trochus, when decorticated, the Turbo exhibits splendid pearly, gold, or silver irridescent colours.

Shell thick, pearly in the interior; depressed, conical, or sub-turreted; umbilicated or not, little or not carinated at its circumference; aperture round or little depressed; the middle of the external edge not bent, but sometimes hollowed or sloped in some part; the edges rarely joined by a callosity; the columella arched, rarely twisted, and not truncated at the base; operculum calcareous or horny; the spire visible externally in the latter and interiorly in the former; the exterior often thickened and curved.

Turbo marmoratus.	Turbo diaphanus.
T. imperialis.	T. rugosus.
T. torquatus.	T. coronatus.

T. sarmaticus.	T. crenulatus.
T. cornutus.	T. hippocastanum.
T. argyrastomus.	T. muricatus.
T. Chrysostomus.	T. littoreus.
T. radiatus.	T. ustulatus.
T. margaritaceus.	T. Nicobaricus.
T. setosus.	T. neritoides.
T. Spenglerianus.	T. retusus.
T. petholatus.	T. rudis.
T. undulatus.	T. obtusatus.
T. pica.	T. pullus.
T. versicolor.	T. cærulescens.
T. smaragdus.	T. cancellatus.
T. cidaris.	T. costatus.

T. pica. The Magpie Turbo. Pl. 24, fig. 6.

Species in which the aperture is oblique; the columella losing itself entirely in its continuation with the margin, the umbilicus always uncovered; colour black and white.

T. setosus. The bristly Turbo.

Thick, transversely and deeply sulcated, longitudinally striated; spire short, volutions rounded, lip crenulated; inside pearly, variegated with white, green, and brown.

T. rugosus. The rough Turbo.

Species of which the aperture is perfectly round in the direction of the axis; the operculum horny.

5. Planaxis. Two species.

Shell marine, generally small, solid, of an oval conical form, oblong, a little sloping in front; columella flattened and truncated anteriorly; right margin furrowed or radiated within, and thickened by a callosity running to its origin; operculum oval, thin, horny, and sub-spiral.

Planaxis sulcata.   Planaxis undulata.

P. sulcata. The furrowed Planaxis. Pl. 27, fig. 4.

Imperforate, furrowed transversely; outer lip crenulated,

and striated internally; colour grayish white, spotted with black, forming oblique longitudinal bands.

6. Phasianella. The Pheasant Snail. Ten species.

This genus of shells is celebrated for the beauty and variety of the colouring, disposed in such a manner as to resemble the plumage of a pheasant.

They are marine shells, many of which are rare and valuable; they possess a very distinctive character, that of a slightly projecting angle running along the columella.

Shell rather thick, oval, smooth, without epidermis, spire pointed; aperture oval, larger in front, with disunited edges; the right sharp; the columella uniting itself a little with the left edge, and offering interiorly a longitudinal callosity; operculum calcareous, oval, oblong, sub-spiral, the summit at one of its extremities.

Phasianella bulimoides.	Phasianella lineata.
P. rubens.	P. nebulosa.
P. variegata.	P. sulcata.
P. elegans.	P. Mauritiana.
P. Peruviana.	P. angulifera.

P. picta. The painted Phasianella. Pl. 24, fig. 2.

Species smooth, oval, glossy, volutions inflated; reddish white, with crimson or reddish brown spots; aperture sub-ovate.

7. Turritella. The Screw Shell. Thirteen species.

This genus is easily distinguished from all screwlike shells by a sinus on the right margin of the aperture, not existing in any other shell of similar form.

Shell marine, turreted, not pearly, rather thin, striated according to the turning of the spire, which is very pointed, and has numerous whorls; aperture rounded; the edges disunited posteriorly; the right extremity thin, and, when perfect, having a light sinus about the middle; operculum, horny.

Turritella duplicata.
T. terebra.
T. imbricata.
T. replicata.
T. fuscata.
T. cornea.
Turritella brevialis.
T. bicingulata.
T. trisulcata.
T. exoleta.
T. carinifera.
T. Australis.
T. Virginiana.

T. bicingulata. The twice-girdled Turritella. Pl. 24, fig. 5.

Species that answers to the above description.

T. terebra. The auger Turritella.

Taper, pointed, acute transverse striæ, the intermediate spaces prominent and acute; white, reddish, or cream coloured.

FAMILY XVI.

CANALIFERA. Eleven genera.

1. Cerithium. Thirty-six species.

A beautiful and numerous genus of turreted shells, with an expanded outer lip and short beak; the greater part are marine; many are found at the mouths of rivers, and a few in lakes, though none can properly be called river shells. In appearance they are like an elongated pyramidal cone, and the spire is at least two thirds the length of the shell. The exterior is seldom smooth, but striated, tuberculated, granulated, or spinous.

Shell more or less turreted, generally tuberculated; aperture small, oval, oblique; the columellar edge hollowed, callous; the right edge sharp, and dilating a little with age; operculum horny, oval, rounded, sub-spiral, and striated.

Cerithium giganteum.
C. palustre.
C. sulcatum.
C. telescopium.
C. ebeninum.
Cerithium erythræonense.
C. muricatum.
C. radula.
C. crassum.
C. decollatum.

T. rhinoceros.
T. cornigera.
T. ceramica.
T. capitellam.
T. mitis.
T. globulus.

T. infundibulum.
T. craticulata.
T. lineata.
T. nassatula.
T. triserialis.
T. variolaris.

T. ocellata.

T. rapa. The turnip Turbinella.
Species fusiform and almost smooth.

T. scolymus. The artichoke Turbinella.
Species turbinated and spinous.

T. infundibulum. The funnel-shaped Turbinella.
Species turreted and fusiform.

T. pyrum. The pear-shaped Turbinella.
Species with spire short, mucronate; apex mammiliform, beak long; columella with four plaits; colour yellowish white, with irregular reddish brown spots.

4. Cancellaria. Twelve species.

This genus is not given by De Blainville precisely like Lamarck, as he has removed those that are greatly canaliculated either to the Murex or Turbinella. They are all marine shells, and greatly approximate the last-mentioned genus.

Shell oval, globular, ventricose, rugged; the spire middling, pointed; aperture ovate, enlarged, grooved, and sometimes sub-canaliculated anteriorly; the right edge effuse, concave, sharp; the left or columellar edge almost straight, and marked in the middle by two or three plaits; operculum horny.

Cancellaria reticulata.
C. asperella.
C. scalaria.
C. scalariformis.
C. nodulosa.
C. cancellata.

Cancellaria senticosa.
C. citharella.
C. spirata.
C. obliquata.
C. rugosa.
C. Ziervogeliana.

C. reticulata. The reticulated Cancellaria. Pl. 25, fig. 5.

Oval, strong, ventricose; columella with three plaits; distant, coarse, reticulated striæ; sometimes with yellow or orange bands; aperture white.

5. Fasciolaria. Eight species.

This genus was separated by Lamarck from the Murex of Linnæus on account of having no varices.

Shell fusiform or sub-fusiform; aperture middling, elongated, almost symmetrical, terminated by a rather long straight tube; external edge sharp; the columellar edge with two or three oblique plaits.

Fasciolaria tulipa.	Fasciolaria coronata.
F. distans.	F. filamentosa.
F. trapezium.	F. ferruginea.
F. aurantiaca.	F. tarentina.

F. tulipa. The tulip Fasciolaria. Pl. 25, fig. 4.
Species fusiform, not tuberculated.

F. trapezium. The striped tower Fasciolaria.
Species fusiform, volutions tuberculated, ventricose; reddish fawn coloured, with transverse double, slightly undulated lines; inside of aperture with reddish striæ.

F. filamentosa. The threaded Fasciolaria.
Species turreted and tuberculated.

6. Fusus. Thirty-six species.

Likewise taken from the Murex; they are marine shells, of an elongated fusiform shape, with whorls ventricose in the middle or at the lower extremity.

Shell covered with epidermis, rough, fusiform, or ventricose in the middle; prolonged behind by the spire, but particularly forward by the canal; aperture oval; the columellar edge straight or nearly so; the exterior edge sharp; operculum oval, horny, with sub-concentric elements, and summit lateral.

Fusus colosseus.	Fusus corona.
F. longissimus.	F. raphanus.
F. colus.	F. filosus.
F. tuberculatus.	F. polygonoides.
F. Nicobaricus.	F. verruculatus.
F. distans.	F. lignarius.
F. torulosus.	F. Syracusanus.
F. incrassatus.	F. strigosus.
F. multicarinatus.	F. varius.
F. sulcatus.	F. crebricostatus.
F. antiquus.	F. Afer.
F. despectus.	F. rubens.
F. carinatus.	F. sinistralis.
F. proboscidiferus.	F. Nifat.
F. Islandicus.	F. articulatus.
F. morio.	F. buccinatus.
F. coronatus.	F. aculeiformis.
F. cochlidium.	F. scalarinus.

F. colus. The spindle Fusus. Pl. 25, fig. 3.

Species turreted or sub-turreted, not umbilicated; outer lip entire, columella smooth.

F. filosus. The threaded Fusus.

Species sub-turreted and umbilicated.

7. Pyrula. Twenty-eight species.

Distinguished from the Fusus by having a short depressed spire, and the last whorl very large and ventricose, giving this shell the shape of a pear.

Shell pyriform by the depression of the spire, the canal conical, very long or middling, sometimes a little sloped; aperture oval, very large; columella smooth.

Pyrula canaliculata.	Pyrula ternatana.
P. carica.	P. bezoar.
P. perversa.	P. rapa.
P. candelabrum.	P. papyracea.

P. tuba.	P. galeodes.
P. bucephala.	P. angulata.
P. vespertilio.	P. squamosa.
P. melongena.	P. nodosa.
P. reticulata.	P. citrina.
P. ficus.	P. abbreviata.
P. ficoides.	P. neritoidea.
P. spirata.	P. deformis.
P. spirillus.	P. lineata.
P. elongata.	P. plicata.

P. melongena. The open-mouth Pyrula. Pl. 25, fig. 6.

Species ventricose, tube or canal short; aperture very large and effuse; tuberculated, striated longitudinally.

P. ficus. The fig Pyrula.

Spire very short; volutions rounded above; very thin and ventricose; colour yellowish brown, with dark brown spots; covered with decussated striæ.

8. Struthiolaria. Two species.

The shells of this genus are marine, inhabited by mollusca, that, by frequently moving in and out of the shell while wandering on the shore in search of food, produce singular callosities on the two edges of the aperture. They generally resemble the Murex and Buccinum, but are distinguished by a thickened marginal lip on the right side.

Shell ovate, spire produced; aperture sinuous, terminated at the base by a very short canal; straight, and without a notch; columellar edge callous and effuse; right edge with a thickened varix.

Struthiolaria nodulosa.   Struthiolaria crenulata.

S. nodulosa. The nodulous Struthiolaria. Pl. 25, fig 1.

Ovate, grooved and striated transversely; top of volutions flattened and nodulous; cream-coloured, with undulated, brownish-yellow longitudinal lines; interior of lip yellowish.

9. Ranella. Fourteen species.

This genus of shells has two rows of varices or thickened bands, arranged on either side in rows, so that it forms a distinct division between the Struthiolaria and the Murex.

Shell oval, as if depressed by the preservation of each side of a longitudinal thickened band; aperture oval, almost symmetrical by the excavation of the columellar edge, terminating anteriorly by a short canal, often a little sloping; a sinus at the posterior junction of the two edges.

Ranella gigantea.	Ranella granulata.
R. leucostoma.	R. granifera.
R. candisata.	R. semigranosa.
R. Argus.	R. bitubercularis.
R. ranina.	R. crumēna.
R. spinosa.	R. anceps.
R. bufonia.	R. pygmæa.

R. ranina. The froglike Ranella. Pl. 25, fig. 2. Species not umbilicated.

R. granulata. The granulated Ranella. Species not umbilicated.

R. spinosa. The prickly Ranella. Species of which the varices have elongated spines; beak sulcated; outer lip internally crenated; acute, short, distinct muricated tubercles; fawn coloured.

10. Murex. The Trumpet Shell. Sixty-six species.

Though so greatly divided by Lamarck, this is a beautiful and numerous genus, comprehending only such shells as have three or more varices on each whorl.

These varices show the number of times the animal has increased the size of its shell, and what proportion is added at each increase.

The shells are generally irregular in form, arising from their surfaces being usually armed with spines, knobs, striæ, or foliations.

Shell generally oval; the spire always but little elevated, armed with longitudinal transverse varices or thickened bands; aperture small; very oval and symmetrical by the excavation of the left edge, formed by a plate applied on the columella, terminated anteriorly by a middling sized canal, sometimes very long and close; the right edge more or less adorned with varices; operculum horny, oval, complete, almost circular, with sub-concentric partitions; summit terminal.

Murex crassispina.	Murex cornutus.
M. Haustellum.	M. brandaris.
M. acanthopterus.	M. ternispina.
M. tenuispina.	M. brevispina.
M. rarispina.	M. tenuirostrum.
M. inflatus.	M. motacilla.
M. elongatus.	M. asperrimus.
M. palmarosæ.	M. phyllopterus.
M. brevifrons.	M. capucinus.
M. calcitrapa.	M. tripterus.
M. adustus.	M. trigonularis.
M. rufus.	M. uncinarius.
M. axicornis.	M. hemitripterus.
M. cervicornis.	M. gibbosus.
M. aculeatus.	M. triqueter.
M. microphyllus.	M. trigonulus.
M. brassica.	M. quadrifrons.
M. saxatilis.	M. turbinatus.
M. endivia.	M. trunculus.
M. radix.	M. anguliferus.
M. melanomathos.	M. melonulus.
M. hexagonus.	M. Magellanicus.
M. scorpio.	M. lamellosus.
M. secundus.	M. erinaceus.
M. Tarentinus.	M. cinguliferus.
M. scaber.	M. subcarinatus.
M. costularis.	M. torosus.

M. polygonulus.	M. lyratus.
M. vitulinus.	M. concatenatus.
M. angularis.	M. granarius.
M. crispatus.	M. fimbriatus.
M. fenestratus.	M. pulchellus.
M. cingulatus.	M. aciculatus.

M. crassispina. The thick-spined Murex. Pl. 26, fig. 3.
Species with tube very long and spiny.

M. adustus. The burnt Murex. Pl. 26, fig. 1.
Species with three ramified varices.

M. Haustellum. The Snipe Murex. Pl. 26, fig. 4.
Species with tube very long, and without spines.

M. acanthopterus. The prickly Murex.
Species with three varices on each whorl.

M. melanomathos. The black-spined Murex.
Species which have whorls with more than three varices; the tube almost close.

M. lyratus. The lyre-shaped Murex.
Species sub-turreted.

M. vitulinus. The young Murex.
Species sub-globular; the spire and the canal rather short, very open; the aperture sub-effuse.

11. Triton. Thirty-one species.

In this genus the varices are in longitudinal rows or series, but alternating, few in number, sometimes only one on each whorl. They are never spinous or foliated, though frequently plaited or tuberculated.

The Triton variegatus type of this genus is one of the largest spiral shells.

Shell oval, with spire and canal straight, middling, generally rough, garnished with varices, rare, scattered, and preserved in longitudinal rows; aperture sub-oval, elongated, terminated by a short, open canal; the columellar edge less hollowed than the right, and covered with a callosity; operculum horny, oval, rounded, and rather large.

Triton variegatus.	Triton pyrum.
T. nodiferus.	T. cynocephalum.
T. Australis.	T. tripus.
T. lampas.	T. canaliferus.
T. scrobiculator.	T. retusus.
T. Spengleri.	T. clavator.
T. corrugatus.	T. tuberosus.
T. succinctus.	T. vespaceus.
T. pilearis.	T. chlorostomus.
T. lotorium.	T. anus.
T. femoralis.	T. clathratus.
T. subdistortus.	T. rubecula.
T. cancellatus.	T. cutaceus.
T. maculosus.	T. dolarius.
T. clandestinus.	T. Tranquebaricus.

T. undosus.

T. variegatus. The trumpet Triton. Pl. 26, fig. 5.

The smoothest species, oblong, ventricose, tubiform; aperture dilated; suture of the spire crenulated; pillar lip grooved obliquely; colour pale purple, clouded and spotted with brown.

T. cutaceus. The rough-skin Triton.

Species with spire rather short, always very tuberculated, often umbilicated; a sinus at the posterior junction of the two edges.

T. anus. The grinning Triton.

Species similar to the T. cutaceus, but having the aperture surrounded by a thin dilated membrane and irregular teeth.

FAMILY XVII.

ALATA. Three genera.

1. Rostellaria. Three species.

Lamarck formed this genus from the Strombus of Linnæus on account of having a sinus in the lower part of the right margin contiguous to the canal. The beak is generally curved, and short in comparison to the length of the spire, but sometimes it is straight, and equal in length to the other part of the shell.

The R. rectirostris is one of the most rare shells known.

Shell sub-depressed, turreted, with spire produced and pointed; aperture oval by the excavation of the columellar edge; the right margin dilating by age, and having a sinus contiguous to the pointed canal which terminates the shell.

Rostellaria curvirostris.   Rostellaria rectirostris.
R. pes-Pelicani.

R. curvirostris. The curved beak Rostellaria. Pl. 27, fig. 2.

Species with the right edge digitated.

R. pes-Pelicani. The Pelican's foot Rostellaria.

Species turreted, with four digitations on the right edge; body and volutions ribbed longitudinally and crowned with papillæ; flesh-coloured or white.

2. Pteroceras. Seven species.

Formed from the Strombus, being distinct from it by not having the canal at the base shortened or truncated. It greatly resembles the Rostellaria, but the sinus of the right margin is distant from the body. From its digitation or long recurved claws it has often been called the Spider Shell.

Shell oblong-ovate, ventricose, canal elongated, attenuated, and often closed; right margin dilating by age into an expanded, digitated wing, attached to and covering a short spire, with a sinus in the lower part not contiguous to the body.

    Pteroceras truncata.   Pteroceras pseudoscorpio.
    P. lambis.   P. scorpio.
    P. millepeda.   P. aurantia.
              P. chiragra.

P. chiragra. The Devil's Claw. Pl. 28, fig. 3.

Tuberculated, with six digitated, canaliculated rays, closed in the adult shell; outer lip internally striated.

P. scorpio. The Scorpion Pteroceras.

Species with digitations on the external edge, varying in number from six to ten.

3. Strombus. The Wing Shell. Thirty-two species.

As now defined and characterized by Lamarck, is easily distinguished by not having the winged aperture on the right side dentated or digitated, and the sinus therein always separated from the canal.

In some species the exterior is variously striated, smooth, wrinkled longitudinally, or tuberculated; the interior presents vivid and beautiful colours.

These shells frequently attain a large size and great solidity.

Shell thick, sub-involute, diconic, or ventricose, terminated like a cone before and behind; aperture very long, narrow, terminated anteriorly by a canal more or less elongated, recurved; the edges parallel; the external dilating with age, offering behind a gutter at its attachment to the spire, and before a sinus more posterior than the canal, through which passes the head of the animal; operculum horny, long, and narrow, with elements as if imbricated; the summit terminal.

    Strombus gigas.   Strombus Canarium.
    S. accipitrinus.   S. Isabella.
    S. latissimus.   S. vittatus.
    S. tricornis.   S. epidromis.

S. gallus.	S. colomba.
S. bituberculatus.	S. succinctus.
S. cristatus.	S. troglodytes.
S. dilatatus.	S. tridentatus.
S. bubonius.	S. urceus.
S. lentiginosus.	S. plicatus.
S. auris-Dianæ.	S. Floridus.
S. pugilis.	S. papilio.
S. pyrulatus.	S. lineatus.
S. gibberulus.	S. marginatus.
S. Luhuanus.	S. turritus.
S. Mauritianus.	S. cancellatus.

S. polyfasciatus. The many-banded Strombus. Pl. 28, fig. 2.

Species distinguished by its bands, and by having the margin of the outer lip thickened.

S. auris-Dianæ. Diana's Ear Strombus.

Oblong-ovate; spire acute, tuberculated, and transversely striated; base recurved, outer lip thick, anterior lobe with a finger-like termination.

S. pugilis. The fighting, or thick-spined Strombus.

Anterior lip prominent, rounded, smooth; spire crowned with spines, the outermost whorl cancellate; columella much reflected; beak three-lobed, obtuse, flesh-coloured, and polished within.

FAMILY XVIII.

PURPURIFERA. Eleven genera.

1. Cassidaria. Five species.

Marine shell, sometimes confounded with the Cassis, but distinguished by the canal which terminates the aperture being ascendant, very little arched, and not suddenly recurved.

Shell sub-globular, ventricose, tuberculated, or fluted; spire short and pointed; aperture long, oval, sub-canaliculated anteriorly; the right edge effuse and folded back; the columella covered over with a broad, smooth callosity, uniting behind to the right edge; operculum horny.

  Cassidaria echinophora. Cassidaria cingulata.
  C. Tyrrhena.   C. striata.
      C. oniscus.

C. echinophora. The tuberculated Cassidaria. Pl. 27, fig. 5.

Species oval, sub-globular, canal sub-ascendant, with tuberculated belts or ribs.

C. Tyrrhena. The Tyrrhenian Cassidaria.

Species ovate, grooved transversely, volutions convex; apex with one tubercle; tawny colour.

2. Cassis. The Helmet Shell. Twenty-five species.

This genus was formed from the Buccinum, from which it is easily distinguished; the latter having only a notch at the base, and the Cassis with a canal abruptly turned towards the back of the shell.

Shell inflated oval, sub-involute, spire very little projecting; aperture long, oval, sometimes very narrow, terminated anteriorly by a very short canal, sloped and recurved obliquely towards the back; the right edge more or less concave, reflected backward, and often dentated within; the columella covered with a large callosity, denticulated or wrinkled in all its length; operculum horny.

  Cassis cornuta.   Cassis crumena.
  C. tuberosa.   C. plicaria.
  C. Madagascariensis. C. areola.
  C. flammea.   C. zebra.
  C. fascinata.   C. decussata.
  C. glauca.   C. abbreviata.
  C. rufa.   C. sulcosa.
  C. pennata.   C. granulosa.
  C. testiculus.   C. saburon.
  C. achatina.   C. canaliculata.

C. pyrum.   C. semigranosa.
C. Ceylanica.   C. vibex.
C. erinaceus.

C. tuberosa. The tuberous Cassis. Pl. 28, fig. 5.
Species in which the aperture is long, the external edge almost straight, and the spire with thickened bands.

C. flammea. The flaming Cassis.
Species in which the aperture is sub-oval, and the external edge excavated; spire short, base triangular; columella rugose; outer lip thickened.

C. areola. The draught-board Cassis.
Smooth, shiny, white, with square orange tesselated spots; spire short and conical, with decussated striæ; lower part of columella rugose.

3. Ricinula. Nine species.

Shell oval or sub-globular, thick, armed with points or tubercles, with a depressed spire; aperture narrow, elongated, notched, sometimes canaliculated anteriorly, and digitated externally; the left edge more or less callous, sometimes denticulated; operculum horny, oval, transverse, with elements slightly imbricated.

Ricinula horrida.   Ricinula digitata.
R. clathrata.   R. pisolina.
R. arachnoidea.   R. aspera.
R. miticula.   R. morus.
R. mutica.

R. horrida. The horrid Ricinula. Pl. 26, fig. 2.
Species without a canal; exterior covered with strong, obtuse black tubercles, with the interstices white, striated transversely; interior rich purple colour; outer lip with five triangular grooved radii, between which at their base the margin is crenulated.

U

R. digitata. The digitated Ricinula.

Species canaliculated; two long palmated digits at the side of the aperture.

4. Purpura. Fifty species.

This genus has its name from the purple liquid produced by the animal, from which the ancients extracted the Tyrian purple die. This is the last genus that presents the appearance of a canal at the base of the aperture, and therefore rightly precedes the remaining genera of this family, all of which are without a canal.

Shell oval, thick, generally tuberculated; spire short; the last whorl much greater than all the others united; aperture oval, greatly dilated, terminated anteriorly by a canal short, oblique, and notched at the extremity; the columellar edge almost straight, covered with a callosity pointed anteriorly; operculum horny, flat, almost semicircular, with transverse striæ slightly marked; the summit behind.

Purpura Persica.	Purpura sacellum.
P. Rudolphi.	P. squamosa.
P. patula.	P. rugosa.
P. collumellaris.	P. textilosa.
P. succincta.	P. sertum.
P. consul.	P. Francolinus.
P. armigera.	P. limbosa.
P. bitubercularis.	P. ligata.
P. hippocastanum.	P. cruentata.
P. undata.	P. lapillus.
P. hæmastoma.	P. imbricata.
P. manicella.	P. lagenaria.
P. bufo.	P. cateracta.
P. callosa.	P. bicostalis.
P. neritoides.	P. plicata.
P. planospira.	P. fiscella.
P. callifera.	P. thiarella.
P. coronata.	P. rustica.

P. carinifera.	P. semi-imbricata.
P. scalariformis.	P. echinulata.
P. hystrix.	P. clavus.
P. deltoidea.	P. fasciolaris.
P. unifascialis.	P. vexillum.
P. retusa.	P. bizonalis.
P. trochlea.	P. nucleus.

P. Persica. The Persian Purpura. Pl. 28, fig. 4.

Transversely sulcated and striated between the ridges; colour burnt-umber, ridges yellowish, with dark brown spots; upper ridge and the superior edges of the volutions mucronate; interior sulcated and striated.

P. lapillus. The common Purpura.

Species small, white, sometimes banded with yellow or brown, with a scaly surface.

5. Monoceros. The Unicorn. Five species.

Derived its name from the long, conical-pointed, somewhat recurved tooth in the outer lip, by which alone it can well be distinguished from the Purpura; and with this characteristic difference the description of the shell of the Purpura will answer for this genus.

Monoceros cingulatum.	Monoceros striatum.
M. imbricatum.	M. glabratum.
M. crassilabrum.	

M. cingulatum. The belted Monoceras.

Cylindrical, columella not smooth, but irregularly plaited or wrinkled, and the tooth does not extend within the interior of the whorls as in the other species, but appears affixed only to the edge of the lip; volutions flattened in their upper edges; transverse spiral brown bands.

6. Concholepas. One species.

Formerly considered a Patella, but distinct from it on account of having an operculum. It is particularly distinguished by having two teeth at the base of the right side.

Shell wide, rough, oval, spire very short, not projecting; aperture very large, oval, effuse, sloped anteriorly; the edges united; the right or external very thick, dentated; the two teeth which limit the slope are a little larger than the others; muscular impression visible, and almost in form of a horse-shoe; operculum horny and rudimentary.

C. Peruvianus. The Peruvian Concholepas. Pl. 28, fig. 1.

The type of this genus; exterior dark brown, interior white.

7. Harpa. The Harp Shell. Eight species.

This genus of shells is truly beautiful; it was classed by Linnæus with the Buccinum, but Lamarck considered that they were, for their beauty, worthy of forming a genus by themselves.

Shell oval, inflated, rather thin, with longitudinal parallel ribs, formed by the preservation of the thickening of the right margin; the spire very short, pointed, the last whorl much longer than all the others together; aperture large, ovate, widely notched anteriorly; the right edge much excavated and thickened outwardly; the columella smooth, and terminated in a point anteriorly.

Harpa imperialis.	Harpa articularis.
H. ventricosa.	H. rosea.
H. conoidalis.	H. minor.
H. nobilis.	H. striata.

H. imperialis. The imperial Harp.

Species in which the number of ribs far exceeds that of any other, and occasions it often to be called the many-ridged harp; a small spiral keel round the summit. A rare and valuable species.

H. nobilis. The noble Harp. Pl. 29, fig. 2.
A regular species.

H. rosea. The roseate Harp.

Oblong-ovate; flesh coloured, with roseate interrupted bands; ribs remote; columella of a fine rosy hue.

8. Dolium. The Tun Shell. Seven species.

The shells of this genus are generally large, thin, and globose, with a wide aperture, and toothed or crenated outer lip; they have a brittle and light structure, and although some of them grow to a very large size, they retain their characteristic fragility and thinness.

Shell sub-globular, very ventricose, thin, encircled by decurrent flutings; the spire very short; the last turn much larger than all the others together; aperture oblong, very large, by the great excavation of the right edge, which is crenated through all its length; columella twisted; operculum unknown.

Dolium galea.	Dolium fasciatum.
D. olearium.	D. pomum.
D. maculatum.	D. variegatum.
	D. perdix.

D. perdix. The Partridge Dolium. Pl. 29, fig. 4.

Species sub-umbilicated, ovate-oblong, thin, thickly ribbed, and convex; colour reddish brown, clouded and spotted with white.

D. galea. The brown Tun.

Species not umbilicated; sometimes exceeds ten inches in diameter.

9. Buccinum. The Whelk. Fifty-eight species.

Notwithstanding the divisions of the Linnæan Buccinum into so many different genera, it still presents a great variety and diversity of species.

Shell slightly covered with epidermis, oval, elongated; the spire middling elevated; aperture oblong, oval, notched, and sometimes sub-canaliculated anteriorly; the right edge thick, not reflected; columella simple and swelled at the upper part; operculum horny, complete, oval, with sub-concentric elements; the summit slightly marked and marginal.

Buccinum undatum.	Buccinum testudineum.
B. glaciale.	B. achatinum.
B. Anglicanum.	B. glans.
B. papyraceum.	B. papillosum.
B. annulatum.	B. olivaceum.
B. lævissimum.	B. canaliculatum.
B. crenulatum.	B. tricarinatum.
B. reticulatum.	B. Brasilianum.
B. Tranquebaricum.	B. semiconvexum.
B. lineatum.	B. fasciolatum.
B. fuscatum.	B. vinosum.
B. lineolatum.	B. tenuiplicatum.
B. maculosum.	B. sub-spinosum.
B. politum.	B. Ascanias.
B. suturale.	B. lævigatum.
B. mutabile.	B. flexuosum.
B. inflatum.	B. aciculatum.
B. retusum.	B. corniculatum.
B. ventricosum.	B. cribrarium.
B. gemmulatum.	B. grana.
B. Coromandelianum.	B. coccinella.
B. fasciatum.	B. zebra.
B. miga.	B. dermestoideum.
B. lyratum.	B. aurantium.
B. arcularia.	B. pedicular.
B. coronatum.	B. gibbolusum.
B. Thersites.	B. pullus.
B. pauperatum.	B. marginulatum.
B. neriteum.	B. polygonatum.

B. undatum. The common Whelk, or waved Buccinum. Species oval, slightly ventricose, and subcarinated on the whorls of the spire; sulcated obliquely; striated transversely and longitudinally; volutions convex; aperture white or yellow; covered with a yellowish epidermis.

B. papillosum. The prickly-lip Buccinum. Pl. 29, fig. 1.

Species with the spire elevated, more or less tuberculated, the edges of the aperture separated posteriorly by a narrow, rather deep sinus; the right dentated anteriorly.

B. reticulatum. The reticulated Buccinum.

Species short, ventricose, sub-globular.

B. achatinum. The Agathine Buccinum.

Species smooth, the spire rather elevated; the aperture wider anteriorly.

10. Eburna. Five species.

Shell oval or elongated, smooth; the spire pointed, its whorls as if rounded; aperture ovate, elongated, effuse, and widely notched anteriorly; the right margin entire; the columella callous posteriorly, umbilicated, sub-canaliculated at its external or right side.

Eburna glabrata.	Eburna spirata.
E. Ceylanica.	E. areolata.

E. lutosa.

E. Ceylanica. The Ceylon Eburna. Pl. 29, fig. 3.

Species smooth, white, with irregular large purplish spots; apex acute, tipped with blue; sutures with an elevated line; umbilicus filled with spines.

11. Terebra. The Needle Shell. Twenty-four species.

This genus of shells is remarkable for their sharp, lengthened, and spiral form, which obtained for them the common name of Needles.

Shell elongated oval, spire pointed, slightly elevated, or sub-turreted; aperture wide, oval, strongly notched anteriorly; lower end of the columella twisted or oblique.

Terebra maculata.	Terebra striatula.
T. flammea.	T. chlorata.
T. crenulata.	T. cerithina.
T. dimidiata.	T. raphanula.

T. muscaria.	T. cingulifera.
T. subulata.	T. myuros.
T. oculata.	T. scabrella.
T. duplicata.	T. strigilata.
T. Babylonia.	T. lanceata.
T. corrugata.	T. aciculina.
T. Senegalensis.	T. granulosa.
T. cærulescens.	T. vittata.

T. Buccinoides. The Buccinum-shaped Terebra. Pl. 27, fig. 3.

Answers to the above description.

T. vittata. The filleted Terebra.

Species smooth, pale fawn coloured; transversely striated, with transverse purplish fillets.

T. maculata. The spotted Terebra. Pl. 27, fig. 1.

Species very long, spire pointed; aperture oval, small, widely notched anteriorly; the external edge thin and sharp, the left with an oblique thickening at its extremity.

FAMILY XIX.

COLUMELLARIA. Five genera.

1. Columbella. Eighteen species.

The shells of this genus are short, small, and rather thick; found in the seas of hot countries.

The C. mercatoria is very common on the shores of the Atlantic in warm latitudes, and was formerly used as money.

Shell thick, turbinated; spire short, obtuse; aperture narrow, elongated, terminated by a very short canal or notch, rendered narrow by an inflation at the inner side of the right edge, and by some plaits on the columella; a very small horny operculum.

Columbella strombiformis.	Columbella flavida.
C. rustica.	C. semipunctata.
C. mercatoria.	C. bizonalis.
C. Hebræa.	C. reticulata.

C. pardalina.	C. fulgurans.
C. scripta.	C. mendicaria.
C. ovulata.	C. turturina.
C. nitida.	C. punctata.
C. zonalis.	C. unifascialis.

C. strombiformis. The Strombus-shaped Columbella. Pl. 29, fig. 6.

The type of this genus, partly characterized by its name.

C. mercatoria. The merchant Columbella.

Ovate, white, sulcated, transversely clouded with brown or yellow; outer lip dentated internally.

2. Mitra. The Mitre Shell. Eighty species.

A numerous and elegant genus of shells, separated by Lamarck from the Voluta on account of possessing several strong distinctive characters. The spire is always pointed, and the columellar plaits, diminishing in size, are always transverse and parallel to each other.

The exterior is sometimes most beautifully marked with transverse grooves, striæ, punctures, or granulations; the colour of almost every hue.

Shell turreted, sub-fusiform, and oval; the spire always pointed at the summit; the aperture small, triangular, wider and strongly notched anteriorly; the external edge sharp, almost straight, always longer than the columella, which is formed by a very thin callosity, and marked with oblique parallel plaits, of which those anterior are the shortest.

Mitra episcopalis.	Mitra pediculus.
M. papalis.	M. lactea.
M. pontificalis.	M. cornicularis.
M. puncticulata.	M. lutescens.
M. millepora.	M. striatula.
M. cardinalis.	M. subulata.
M. archiepiscopalis.	M. cornea.
M. versicolor.	M. tringa.
M. sanguinolenta.	M. melaniana.

M. ferruginea.	M. scutulata.
M. terebralis.	M. dactylus.
M. adusta.	M. fenestrata.
M. granulosa.	M. crenulata.
M. crocata.	M. texturata.
M. casta.	M. conulus.
M. nexilis.	M. limbifera.
M. olivaria.	M. aurantiaca.
M. scabriuscula.	M. amphorella.
M. granatina.	M. coronata.
M. crenifera.	M. paupercula.
M. serpentina.	M. cucumerina.
M. tæniata.	M. patriarchalis.
M. plicaria.	M. muriculata.
M. corrugata.	M. torulosa.
M. costellaris.	M. ebenus.
M. lyrata.	M. harpæformis.
M. melongena.	M. semifasciata.
M. cinctella.	M. retusa.
M. vulpecula.	M. microzonias.
M. Caffra.	M. ficulina.
M. sanguisuga.	M. nucleola.
M. stigmataria.	M. unifascialis.
M. filosa.	M. bacillum.
M. fissurata.	M. conularis.
M. arenosa.	M. plumbea.
M. clavulus.	M. larva.
M. literata.	M. pisolina.
M. Peronii.	M. dermestina.
M. obliquata.	M. granulifera.
M. oniscina.	M. tabanula.

M. episcopalis. The episcopal Mitre. Pl. 31, fig. 7.
Species turreted, with spiral whorls very wide and entire; the aperture effuse anteriorly.

M. papalis. The papal Mitre.
Species with coronated whorls.

M. pontificalis. The pontifical Mitre.

Species covered with a yellowish epidermis, beneath which are interrupted fillets of orange coloured spots; spire crowned with tubercles.

M. micozonias. The small white-banded Mitre.

Species sub-ovate, spire very short, generally tubercled.

M. dactylus. The six-plaited Mitre.

Species oval, spire very short, and generally latticed.

M. tæniata. The riband Mitre.

Species flaring, turreted, ribbed; spire more than half the length of the shell; aperture very narrow, long, subcanaliculated, with one plait.

3. Voluta. The Volute or Wreath. 44 species.

This genus, as established by Linnæus, included shells of different families, promiscuously blended together, rendering it difficult to determine satisfactorily respecting shells under examination. As arranged and classified by Lamarck, it is still a numerous and beautiful genus, containing some of the most rare and costly shells, particularly V. Junonia or Peacock Volute, of which very few are known. They vary considerably in size; some are very minute, and others large; they are found chiefly in the seas of the torrid zone or southern hemisphere.

Shell oval, more or less ventricose; the first whorls of the spire mamillose; aperture in general much more long than wide, strongly and obliquely notched anteriorly; the right edge a little reflected, entire; the columellar edge excavated, and adorned with great plaits, more or less oblique, and a little variable in number with age.

Voluta nautica.	Voluta Neptuni.
V. diadema.	V. cymbium.
V. armata.	V. olla.
V. ducalis.	V. proboscidalis.
V. tesselata.	V. porcina.

V. Æthiopica.	V. scapha.
V. melo.	V. Brasiliana.
V. imperialis.	V. mitis.
V. pellis-serpentis.	V. nivosa.
V. vespertilio.	V. serpentina.
V. Hebræa.	V. thiarella.
V. musica.	V. carneolata.
V. chlorosina.	V. Guinaica.
V. lævigata.	V. fulva.
V. polyzonalis.	V. sulcata.
V. nodulosa.	V. nucleus.
V. magnifica.	V. undulata.
V. ancilla.	V. lapponica.
V. Magellanica.	V. vexillum.
V. Pacifica.	V. volvacea.
V. fulminata.	V. festiva.
V. Junonia.	V. mitræformis.

V. Æthiopica. The Æthiopian Volute. Pl. 30, fig. 2.

Species large, oval, convex, ventricose; spire papillary, with whorls coronated with elevated hollow spines.

V. musica. The music Volute.

Species oval, marked like musical notes set in scores on its surface; spire sub-tuberculated.

V. Magellanica. The Magellan Volute.

Species sub-fusiform, elongated, and sub-turreted; no spines or tubercles on the whorls.

4. Marginella. Twenty-four species.

Distinguished from the Voluta, from which it was taken, by having the outer lip thickened.

Shell smooth, polished, ovate, oblong, sub-conic, spire short and papillary; aperture narrow, sub-ovate, by a light curve of the right edge, which is inflated or reflected, slightly notched anteriorly; the columellar edge marked with three distinct oblique plaits.

Marginella glabrella.	Marginella nubeculata.
M. radiata.	M. cærulescens.
M. quinqueplicata.	M. aurantia.
M. limbata.	M. bivaricosa.
M. rosea.	M. longivaricosa.
M. lifasciata.	M. muscaria.
M. faba.	M. eburnea.
M. dentifera.	M. formicula.
M. dactylus.	M. persicula.
M. bullata.	M. lineata.
M. cornea.	M. tessellata.
M. avellana.	M. interrupta.

M. lineata. The lineated Marginella. Pl. 30, fig. 3.

Species with aperture as long as the shell; spire not projecting, sometimes sunk or umbilicated.

M. faba. The Bean Marginella.

Species with aperture shorter than the shell, and the spire projecting.

M. cærulescens. The cerulean Marginella.

Species with surface bluish white; spire short and acute; four plaits on the columella; interior lip brownish purple.

5. Volvaria. Five species.

The connecting genus between those shells that have a columella and those that are evolved upon their own axis. Distinguished from the Marginella by not having a thickened outer lip. The shells are marine, and generally very small.

Shell cylindrical, convolute; spire obsolete or concealed; aperture narrow, the whole length of the shell, with one or more plaits on the columella at the lower part.

Volvaria monilis.	Volvaria triticea.
V. pallida.	V. oryza.
V. miliacea.	

V. monilis. The Necklace Volvaria. Pl. 29, fig. 5.

Species greatly involuted; aperture very narrow and very

long; plaits on the anterior part of the columellar edge; the exterior edge thin.

FAMILY XX.
Convoluta. Six genera.
1. Ovula. The Egg. 12 species.

This is the first genus of Lamarck's arrangement of convoluted shells; it is nearly allied to the Cypræa, but easily distinguished from it by the want of spire, and by not having teeth on the columellar lip; the right lip is reflected inwardly, sometimes wrinkled and sometimes smooth.

Shell oblong, convex, resembling the Cypræa in form, with the two extremities of the aperture notched, and more or less prolonged like a tube; the left margin dentated.

Ovula oviformis.	Ovula lactea.
O. angulosa.	O. carnea.
O. verrucosa.	O. triticea.
O. hordacea.	O. gibbosa.
O. spelta.	O. acicularis.
O. birostris.	O. volva.

O. volva. The Weaver's Shuttle. Pl. 34, fig. 4.

Species in which the right edge is not thickened or dentated, and with each extremity elongated, producing a long, straight tube, which increases with age. One of the most rare shells of this genus.

O. oviformis. The egg-shaped Ovula. Pl. 34, fig. 1.

Species ovate, much inflated, ventricose in the centre, very glossy and white; right edge dentated, the tube of each extremity very prominent; interior of aperture reddish purple.

O. gibbosa. The belted Ovula. Pl. 34, fig. 2.

Species gibbous, neither end dentated; tubes little marked, and with the body of the shell encircled by a blunt keel.

O. verrucosa. The warty Ovula. Pl. 34, fig. 3.

Species in which the right end is dentated, with a notch and a knob

2. Cypræa. The Cowrie. 68 species.

This genus derived its name from the Cyprian goddess, on account of the beauty of its polished shells. They are generally smooth, of great brilliancy of colour, and elegantly marked with dots, zigzag lines, undulations, or stripes, and covered with an enamel-like glaze. They are found buried in the sand at the bottom of the sea, and are covered by the animal with a thin membrane, which preserves the polish and prevents other testaceous bodies from adhering to them. This membrane consists of two parts, and arises on both sides of the shell in the form of wings, furnishing the testaceous and colouring matter; in some species they do not quite meet on the back of the shell, and the uncovered space is marked by a coloured dorsal line; when these membranous wings overlap each other, this line is nearly obsolete.

These shells often differ much with age; at first in thickness, then because the edges are thin, sharp, hardly dentated, unless internally; and, lastly, sometimes in the outline; this is because the two lobes of the mantle, by turning over the primitive shell during the creeping of the animal, deposite new calcareous matter. De Blainville cannot admit the hypothesis of Bruguiere, that these animals can completely abandon their shell to form a new one.

Shell, when full grown and mature, is solid, oval, convex, very smooth, involute; the spire entirely posterior, very small, often concealed by a calcareous layer deposited by the lobes of the mantle, leaving in some species a small cavity like an umbilicus; aperture longitudinal, very narrow, slightly curved, as long as the shell, with edges internally dentated, and notched at each extremity.

Shell, when young and immature, is very thin, the edges of the aperture not dentated; the right margin sharp and not reflected.

| Cypræa cerina. | Cypræa tigris. |
| C. exanthema. | C. tigrina. |

C. Argus.
C. testudinaria.
C. Mauritiana.
C. mappa.
C. Arabica.
C. histrio.
C. scurra.
C. rattus.
C. stercoraria.
C. mus.
C. ventriculus.
C. Aurora.
C. lynx.
C. adusta.
C. erosa.
C. caurica.
C. Isabella.
C. ocellata.
C. cribraria.
C. turdus.
C. olivacea.
C. stolida.
C. hirundo.
C. undata.
C. zigzag.
C. flaveola.
C. sanguinolenta.
C. poraria.
C. ursellus.
C. asellus.
C. moniliaris.
C. stercus-muscarum.

C. talpa.
C. carneola.
C. lurida.
C. vitellus.
C. caput-serpentis.
C. cinerea.
C. zonata.
C. sordida.
C. icterina.
C. miliaris.
C. variolaria.
C. rufa.
C. cicercula.
C. lota.
C. globulus.
C. ovulata.
C. helvola.
C. Arabicula.
C. staphylæa.
C. pustulata.
C. nucleus.
C. limacina.
C. moneta.
C. obvelata.
C. annulus.
C. radians.
C. oniscus.
C. pediculus.
C. oryza.
C. coccinella.
C. Australis.
C. albella.

C. exanthema. The measly Cypræa.

Species oblong-ovate, brown, with round white spots; dorsal line grayish; marginal teeth brown; spire not quite concealed.

C. Pantherina. The Panther Cypræa. Pl. 31, fig. 4.
Species regular, beautifully spotted like a panther.

3. Terebellum. One species.

Shell convolute, thin, shining, sub-cylindrical, pointed behind, truncated before; aperture longitudinal, edges entire, columella truncated.

T. subulatum. The awl-shaped Terebellum. Pl. 31, fig. 3.

Answers to the above description, being the only living species known.

4. Ancillaria. Four species.

An intermediate genus between the Terebellum and the Oliva; distinguished from the former by a callous oblique band at the base of the columella; and from the latter by not having the spiral whorls separated by a groove.

Shell smooth, oval, oblong, pointed behind, enlarged and truncated before; the columella covered anteriorly by a callous oblique band; the right lip obtuse.

| Ancillaria cinnamomea. | Ancillaria marginata. |
| A. ventricosa. | A. candida. |

A. cinnamomea. The cinnamon Ancillaria. Pl. 30, fig. 5.

Species with spire nearly obsolete; shell chestnut colour, with white bands; varix of the columella reddish and somewhat striated.

5. Oliva. The Olive. Sixty-two species.

An oval, involuted, internal shell, distinguished from the Ancillaria by a narrow canal continued from its upper angle around the sutures of the spiral whorls. It was formerly classed with the Voluta, which genus has not the canal, so that they cannot be mistaken for each other. There is a callosity uniting with the spiral canal, and another at the base of the columella.

Shell thick, solid, smooth, oval, elongated, sub-cylindrical;

the spiral whorls very small, separated by a canal; aperture long, narrow; the columellar edge reflected anteriorly by a callosity, and striated obliquely through all its length. The shells are generally clouded or covered with waved lines of a brownish colour, more or less dark.

Oliva porphyria.	Oliva reticularis.
O. textilina.	O. flammulata.
O. erythrostoma.	O. granitella.
O. pica.	O. araneosa.
O. tremulina.	O. literata.
O. angulata.	O. scripta.
O. maura.	O. tricolor.
O. sepulturalis.	O. sanguinolenta.
O. fulminans.	O. mustelina.
O. irisans.	O. lugubris.
O. elegans.	O. funebralis.
O. episcopalis.	O. glandiformis.
O. venulata.	O. Peruviana.
O. guttata.	O. Senegalensis.
O. leucophæa.	O. fusiformis.
O. undata.	O. auricularis.
O. inflata.	O. acuminata.
O. bicincta.	O. subulata.
O. harpularia.	O. luteola.
O. hepatica.	O. testacea.
O. ustulata.	O. hiatula.
O. avellana.	O. obtusaria.
O. tessellata.	O. Ceylanica.
O. carneola.	O. nebulosa.
O. espidula.	O. fabagina.
O. oriola.	O. conoidalis.
O. candida.	O. undatella.
O. volutella.	O. eburnea.
O. tigrina.	O. nana.
O. Brasiliana.	O. zonalis.
O. utriculus.	O. oryza.

O. subulata. The awl-shaped Olive. Pl. 30, fig 1.
Species elongated, with very projecting spire.

O. undata. The waved Olive. Pl. 30, fig. 4.
Species oval, spire hardly projecting.

O. cruenta. The bloody Olive.
Species cylindrical, suture canal deep; fawn colour, with triangular spots of purple, and two dark brown spots on the edge of the outer lip.

6. Conus. The Cone. One hundred and eighty-one species.

A genus valued on account of the beauty, symmetry, and variety of its species; some of its shells are very rare and remarkable for their richness of colouring; some are coronated, and others have a plain spire. They are all covered with an epidermis, beneath which is generally a smooth surface, with sometimes a high polish; a few are granulated and tuberculated. They are found in great abundance in the seas of warm climates.

Shell conic, covered with a membranous periosteum, thick, solid, involuted; the summit of the cone anterior; the spire little or not at all projecting; aperture longitudinal, very narrow, turning towards its anterior extremity; the external edge straight, with oblique plaits in its anterior part; operculum very small and horny, sub-spiral, with summit terminal.

Conus marmoreus.
C. Bandanus.
C. nocturnus.
C. Nicobaricus.
C. araneosus.
C. zonatus.
C. imperialis.
C. fuscatus.
C. viridulus.
C. ragius.

Conus tulipa.
C. geographicus.
C. punctatus.
C. tæniatus.
C. musicus.
C. miliaris.
C. mus.
C. lividus.
C. Barbadensis.
C. roseus.

C. cedo-nulli.
C. aurantius.
C. nebulosus.
C. minimus.
C. sulcatus.
C. Hebræus.
C. vermiculatus.
C. arenatus.
C. pulicarius.
C. fustigatus.
C. obesus.
C. varius.
C. millepunctatus.
C. literatus.
C. eburneus.
C. tesselatus.
C. generalis.
C. Maldivus.
C. Malacanus.
C. lineatus.
C. monile.
C. centurio.
C. vitulinus.
C. vulpinus.
C. flavidus.
C. virgo.
C. daucus.
C. pastinaca.
C. capitaneus.
C. classiarius.
C. vittatus.
C. mustelinus.
C. vexillum.
C. Sumatrensis.
C. figulinus.
C. quercinus.

C. cardinalis.
C. Magellanicus.
C. distans.
C. pontificalis.
C. Caledonicus.
C. sponsalis.
C. puncturatus.
C. Ceylanensis.
C. lamellosus.
C. pusillus.
C. exiguus.
C. asper.
C. hyæna.
C. miles.
C. ammiralis.
C. genuanus.
C. papilionaceus.
C. Siamensis.
C. Prometheus.
C. glaucus.
C. Suratensis.
C. monachus.
C. ranunculus.
C. anemone.
C. achatinus.
C. cinereus.
C. stramineus.
C. zebra.
C. lacteus.
C. cingulatus.
C. vicarius.
C. mercator.
C. ochraceus.
C. betulinus.
C. Mediterraneus.
C. puncticulatus.

C. Proteus.
C. leoninus.
C. augur.
C. pertusus.
C. nivosus.
C. fulgurans.
C. acuminatus.
C. amadis.
C. Janus.
C. flammeus.
C. lithoglyphus.
C. testudinarius.
C. venulatus.
C. quæstor.
C. muscosus.
C. Narcissus.
C. Mozambicus.
C. Guinaicus.
C. Franciscanus.
C. informis.
C. rattus.
C. Jamaicensis.
C. amabilis.
C. Omaicus.
C. nobilis.
C. aurisiacus.
C. terminus.
C. striatus.
C. gubernator.
C. granulatus.
C. terebra.
C. verulosus.
C. raphanus.
C. magus.
C. spectrum.
C. bullatus.

C. Mauritianus.
C. fumigatus.
C. eques.
C. luzonicus.
C. catus.
C. verrucosus.
C. acutangulus.
C. mindanus.
C. Japonicus.
C. pusio.
C. columba.
C. madurensis.
C. nemocanus.
C. cancellatus.
C. fusiformis.
C. cærulescens.
C. Aurora.
C. Taitensis.
C. Adansonii.
C. tinianus.
C. Portoricanus.
C. crocatus.
C. strigatus.
C. glans.
C. mitratus.
C. nussatella.
C. aulicus.
C. auratus.
C. colubrinus.
C. clavus.
C. auricomus.
C. omaria.
C. rubiginosus.
C. pennaceus.
C. prælatus.
C. panniculus.

C. cervus.	C. archiepiscopus.
C. stercus-muscarum.	C. canonicus.
C. Timorensis.	C. episcopus.
C. nimbosus.	C. abbas.
C. dux.	O. legatus.
C. tendineus.	C. textilis.
C. præfectus.	C. pyramidalis.
C. melancholicus.	C. gloria-maris.

C. Australis.

C. textilis. The embroidered Cone. Pl. 31, fig. 2.

Species ovate, slightly elongated; the spire rather projecting, pointed, not coronated.

C. imperialis. The imperial Cone.

Species conic, spire coronated, projecting, or flat.

C. striatus. The striated Cone.

Species oblong-ovate, gibbous, not coronated, clouded and strongly striated transversely.

C. generalis. The general Cone.

Species conic, spire projecting, not crowned with tubercles; colour reddish brown, or clouded with orange and interrupted fillets.

C. mustelinus. The Weasel Cone. Pl. 31, fig. 1.

Species with base sub-truncated; spire channelled and banded with orange spots; body whitish, encircled in the middle by orange-spotted bands.

FAMILY XXI.

NAUTILACEA. Two genera.

1. Spirula. One species.

An involute, symmetrical, discoid shell, whose whorls do not touch each other; the septa or partitions are brilliant pearl, concave externally, pierced by a tube called the siphon or siphuncle, placed close to the inner edge of the aperture; covered with a thin epidermis.

S. Peronii. Peron's Spirula. Pl. 36, fig. 2.

Answers to the above description; colour yellowish white.

2. Nautilus. Two species.

An elegant, well-known shell, more or less ventricose, discoid, slightly compressed, umbilicated or not, but never papillose; the septa simple, transverse, not visible externally, the last deeply sunk and perforated by a siphon running through them all; edges entire.

The N. Pompilius, when dissected, displays its beautiful pearly chambers; fine specimens are often converted into drinking-cups by the Orientals, who sometimes remove the outer coating, so that its whole appearance is pearly.

The Nautilis varies in size; some are microscopic; and although they have received different names, and on account of the animal have been made to form different genera, it was deemed unnecessary to treat of them here.

Nautilus Pompilius.   Nautilus umbilicatus.

N. Pompilius. The Pompilius Nautilus. Pl. 36, fig. 3.

Species not umbilicated; the back rounded; aperture round and pearly; siphon sub-central; pale yellow, with chestnut streaks and undulations.

N. umbilicatus. The umbilicated Pompilius. Pl. 36, fig. 1.

Species umbilicated, sub-orbicular; pale fawn colour, with chestnut undated transverse clouds.

FAMILY XXII.

HETEROPODA. Two genera.

1. Argonauta. The Paper Sailor. Three species.

The shells of this genus are remarkable for their fragility, delicacy, and elegance; they resemble a scroll, ornamented with various canaliculated grooves from the summit to the margin, which is bicarinated. The colour is usually bluish, but the keel is of a darker hue; they vary greatly in size.

Shell navicular, symmetrical, very thin, compressed, bicarinated, sub-involuted longitudinally in the same plane; aperture very large, entire, symmetrical, square in front, slightly modified by the turn of the summit, and provided on each side with an earlike appendage, with thick and smooth edges; lips sharp.

 Argonauta argo.   Argonauta tuberculosa.
     A. nitida.

A. argo. The Portuguese man-of-war. Pl. 35, fig. 1.

Characterized above; shell whitish, fragile, keel rather narrow, with sharp-pointed tuberculations; sides striated transversely, wrinkled longitudinally.

A. tuberculosa. The tuberculated Argonaut. Pl. 35, fig. 2.

Species more convex at the sides, with nodulous elevations; keel broader, points more obtuse.

2. Carinaria. The glassy Nautilus. Three species.

In form and texture greatly resembling the Argonauta, but distinguished by only having one keel on the whole length of the back.

Shell symmetrical, carinated or not, very thin, slightly compressed, without spire, but with the summit slightly recurved posteriorly; aperture oval and very entire.

 Carinaria vitrea.   Carinaria fragilis.
     C. cymbium.

C. vitrea. The glassy Carinaria.

Species very rare and beautiful, thin, papyraceous, very fragile and semitransparent; a serrated keel rises up its front, and the sides are decorated with ribs parallel to the base.

C. fragilis. The fragile Carinaria.

Species smaller, very thin, striated longitudinally, diverging from the summit to the margin; no keel.

C. cymbium. The minute Carinaria.

Species not larger than a grain of sand.

GLOSSARY

OF TERMS USED IN CONCHOLOGY.

A.

Abbreviated, shortened, cut short.
Abdomen, the belly.
Aculeated, furnished with, or ending in, prickles.
Acuminated, ending in a sharp point, sharp pointed.
Adnate, adhering or growing together, adjoining.
Alated, winged, applied to the expanded lip of the Strombus genus, &c.
Ambitus, the circumference or outline of the valves.
Annulated, formed or divided into distinct rings.
Annulations, rings.
Antiquated, longitudinally furrowed, but interrupted by transverse furrows, as if the shell had acquired new growth at each furrow.
Aperture, the mouth or opening of the shell.
Apex, the tip or point of the spire.
Apophysis, an excrescence.
Approximating, approaching near to, or near together.
Arcuated, bent in the form of an arch.
Arcuations, bendings, curvings.
Area, the surface contained between lines or boundaries.
Arenose, sandy.
Areola, a small area or circle.
Articulations, junctures, or joinings.
Ascititious, supplemental, additional.
Attenuated, thin, slender.
Aurated, eared, having ears as in the scallops.
Auricled, having appendages like ears.
Auriform, ear-shaped.

B.

Barb, anything that grows in place of a beard.
Base, in univalves, that part of the shell by which it is affixed to rocks, &c., and in multivalves the opposite extremity to the apex. In univalves, the opposite end to the apex.

Beak, the continuation of the body of univalves in which the canal is situated.
Beard, the process by which some bivalves adhere to rocks, &c.
Bellying, distended in the middle.
Bi, prefixed to any word, signifies two.
Biangulated, having two corners or angles.
Bicuspid, having two points.
Bidentate, having two teeth.
Bifid, opening with a cleft.
Bifarious, parting in opposite directions.
Bilabiate, furnished both with an outer and inner lip.
Bilobate, divided into two lobes.
Bimarginate, furnished with a double margin as far as the lip.
Biradiate, having two rays.
Bivalve, consisting of two valves or divisions.
Blotched, spotted in an irregular way.
Blunt, obtuse, opposed to acute.
Borer, a piercer.
Brinded, streaked.
Bulging, gibbous, swollen out.
Bullate, of a blistered appearance.
Byssus, a beard, common in the Mytilus and Pinna.

C.

Calcareous, relating to lime, of a limy nature.
Callosity, a protuberance.
Callus, is composed of two short ribs, united at the base, and converging at the apex towards the hinder part of the shell.
Campanulate, bell-shaped.
Canaliculated, made like a pipe or gutter.
Cancellated, longitudinally and transversely ribbed.
Carinate, having a longitudinal prominence like the keel of a vessel.
Carinated, keeled.
Cartilage, a flexible fibrous substance

by which the valves are united, situated near the beak.
Cauda, the elongated base of the venter, lip, and columella.
Cicatrix, the glossy impression in the inside of the valves, to which the muscles of the animal are affixed.
Ciliate, edged with parallel hairs, bristles, or appendages, like the eyelids.
Cinereous, of ash colour, of the colour of wood ashes.
Clavate, club-shaped, thicker towards the top, elongated towards the base.
Cochleæ, shells of one piece, univalves.
Cochleate, twisted like a screw or the shell of a snail.
Columella, the upright pillar in the centre of most of the univalve shells.
Commissure, a joint or seam.
Complicated, doubled together.
Compressed, perpendicularly squeezed together, in opposition to depressed, which is horizontally flattened.
Concamerated, arched over, vaulted.
Concamerations, divided into compartments, as in the Nautili.
Concave, hollowed out like a bowl.
Concentric, running to a centre.
Conchæ, shells consisting of two or more pieces or valves, bivalves, or multivalves.
Cone, the form of a sugar-loaf.
Confluent, running together.
Conoid, a figure like a cone, sugar-loaf-shaped.
Contorted, twisted, or incumbent on each other, in an oblique direction.
Contracted, shortened, shrunk up.
Convoluted, rolled upon itself, twisted spirally, like a piece of paper rolled between the finger and thumb.
Cordate, heart-shaped.
Cordiform, resembling the form of a heart.
Coriaceous, of a leather-like consistence.
Corneous, of a horn colour, resembling a horn.
Coronal, relating to the crown or top.
Coronated, crowned, or girt towards the apex.
Costated, ribbed, having large ribs.
Corpus, the body of the shell, the last or great wreath in which the aperture is situated.
Cortex, the anterior skin or epidermis.
Crenulated, notched at the margin, scalloped.

Crispated, rough with waving lines.
Cuneiform, shaped like a wedge.
Cylindrical, round like a cylinder or a roller.
Cymbyform, boat-shaped.

D.

Decorticated, worn, divested of epidermis or skin.
Decussated, generally applied to striæ or lines which are crossed, or which intersect each other perpendicularly or horizontally.
Deflexed, bent aside.
Dentary, of or belonging to the teeth.
Dentile, a small tooth, such as the tooth of a saw.
Denticulated, set with small teeth, as in the Arca.
Depressed, pressed down horizontally, low, shallow, flat.
Dexter valve, is the right valve.
Diaphanous, transparent, clear, pellucid.
Digitated, fingered or clawed, as in the lobes of the outer lip of the Strombi, &c.
Disk, the middle part of the valves, or that which lies between the umbo and the margin.
Divaricated, straddling, spreading out widely.
Divergent, tending to various parts or directions from one point.
Dorsum, the back; it generally means the upper surface of the body of the shell, when laid upon the aperture or opening. In the genera of Patella and Haliotis, the back means the upper convex surface.
Dotted, punctured like a thimble.
Duplicated, divided into plaits or folds.
Duplicature, a fold, anything doubled.

E.

Echinated, bristled like a hog, set with spines.
Effuse, spread out.
Elliptical, having the form of an ellipsis, oval.
Elongated, lengthened, drawn out.
Emarginate, } with the edge or margin notched.
Emarginated, }
Ensiform, sabre-shaped.
Entire, whole, uninterrupted, not divided.
Epidermis, the outer coating or scarf-skin of the shell.

GLOSSARY.

Equidistant, being at the same distance.
Equilateral, having all sides alike.
Equivalve, having both valves of equal dimensions.
Exolete, worn or faded.
Exserted, standing out, protruding.
Extraneous, not belonging to a particular thing.

F.

Falcated, bent or hooked like a scythe.
Fasciated, filleted, or covered with bands.
Fascicled, clustered together as in a bundle.
Fasciculated, consisting of little bundles.
Fastigate, flat and even at top.
Faux, what can be seen of the cavity of the first chamber of the shell, by looking in at the aperture.
Ferruginous, of an iron colour, or rust coloured.
Filament, a slender threadlike process.
Filiform, thread-shaped, slender, and of equal thickness.
Fimbriated, fringed.
Fissure, a cleft, a little slit, or narrow chasm.
Flexuous, zigzag, with angles gently winding.
Flexure, a bending.
Fluviatic, of or belonging to a river.
Fluviatile, belonging to fresh water.
Foliaceous, consisting of laminæ or leaves.
Foliated, bent into laminæ or leaves.
Fornix, the excavated part under the umbo. It likewise signifies the upper, or convex shell in the *Ostrea*.
Fragile, brittle, easily broken.
Front, in univalves, when the aperture is turned towards the observer.
Furcated, forked.
Furrow, a small trench or hollow.
Fuscated, darkened, obscured.
Fusiform, spindle-shaped, intermediate between the conical and oval.

G.

Gap, an opening in bivalves when the valves are shut as in the *Pholades*, *Mya*, &c.
Geminated, marked with a double elevated striæ connecting the wreaths.
Geniculate, keeled.
Genus, an assemblage of species possessing certain characters in common, by which they are distinguished from all others.
Genera, the plural of genus.
Gibbous, bulged or bulging.
Glabrous, smooth, having a smooth surface.
Globose, globular.
Granulated, beaded, in small grains or beads.
Groove, a hollow channel.

H.

Hemispherical, in the shape of a half globe.
Hirsute, rough, beset with strong hairs.
Heteroclitical, synonymous with heterostrophe.
Heterostrophe, reversed, applied to shells whose spires turn in a contrary direction to the usual way.
Hispid, hairy.

I & J.

Jagged, denticulated, uneven, toothed like a saw.
Imbricate, placed like the tiles of a house.
Imperforated, not pierced with a hole, wanting an umbilicus.
Inequilateral, when the anterior and posterior sides make different angles with the hinge.
Inequivalve, where one valve is more convex than the other, or dissimilar in other respects, as in the common oyster.
Inarticulate, indistinct, not properly formed.
Incumbent, one lying over the other.
Incurved, } bent inward, crooked.
Incurvated,
Indented, unequally marked, hollowed.
Inflated, tumid, swollen, as if blown out.
Inflected, bent inward.
Inflexed, bent towards each other.
Intercostal, placed between the ribs.
Internode, the space between one knot or joint and another.
Interrupted, divided, separated.
Interstice, space between one part and another, a crevice.
Intortion, the turning or twisting in any particular direction.
Involucre, a covering.
Involution, that part which involves or inwraps another.

Involute, where the exterior lip is turned inward at the margin, as in the Cyprea.
Isabella-colour, a brownish yellow with a shade of brownish red.
Juncture, the joining of the whorl in univalve shells.

K.

Keel, the longitudinal prominence in the Argonauta.
Knob, a protuberance, any part bluntly arising above the rest.

L.

Labra, the lips.
Laciniate, jagged or cut into irregular segments.
Lacunose, having the surface covered with pits.
Lamellar, consisting of films on plates.
Lamellated, divided into distinct plaits or foliations.
Laminæ, thin plates, laid one coat above another.
Lanceolate, oblong, and gradually tapering like the head of a lance.
Lateral, extending to one side from the centre.
Latticed, having longitudinal lines or furrows, decussate by transverse ones.
Lenticulate, doubly convex, of the form of a lens.
Ligament, a solid body, softer than a cartilage, but harder than a membrane, which connects the valves in bivalves.
Limb, the margin of bivalve shells.
Linear, composed of lines.
Lineate, marked with lines.
Lip, the outer edge of the aperture of univalves.
Littoral, of or belonging to the shore.
Lobated, rounded at the edges.
Longitudinal, the length of the shell from the apex to the base.
Lubricity, slipperiness, smoothness of surface.
Lunated, formed like a half moon.
Lunulated, crescent-shaped.
Lunule, a crescent-like mark or spot, situated near the anterior and posterior slopes in bivalve shells.
Luniform, in the shape of a crescent.

M.

Margin, the whole circumference or outline of the shell in bivalves.
Marginated, having a prominent margin or border.
Membrane, a web of several sorts of fibres.
Membranaceous, consisting of membranes.
Mottled, clouded or spotted with various colours.
Mucronate, ending in a sharp rigid point.
Multilocular, many-chambered, consisting of several divisions.
Muricated, clothed with sharp spines.

N.

Nacred, pearly, pearlaceous.
Nemoral, of or belonging to a wood.
Nited, glossy.
Nodose, knotty.
Nucleus, a kernel.

O.

Ob, prefixed to words, is used for inversely or inverted; as *obconic*, inversely conic; *obcordate*, inversely heart-shaped.
Oblong-ovate, egg-shaped or oval.
Obsolete, indistinct, not well defined.
Ocellated, applied to eyelike spots.
Ochreous, of the colour of yellow ochre.
Offuscated, darkened, clouded, dimmed.
Olivaceous, being of a greenish olive colour.
Operculum, a lid which closes the aperture of some turbinated univalves; and also some of the tops of multivalves.
Orbicular, spherical, circular, round.
Order, the second division of the animal kingdom. Orders are made up of a plurality of genera.
Orifice, an opening or perforation.
Ovate, shaped like the longitudinal section of an egg.
Ovoid, oval.

P.

Palmated, webbed, as in the feet of some water-birds.
Papillæ, small dots or pimples.
Papillary, } having the surface covered with dots or pimples.
Papillous, }
Papillose, pimpled, dotted.
Papyraceous, thin as paper.
Parasitical, living on some other body.
Patulous, with a gap or opening.
Pearlaceous, of or like mother-of-pearl.

Partitions, calcareous processes, dividing the shells of the genus Nautilus, Serpula, &c.
Pectinated, resembling the teeth of a comb.
Pedicle, the support of the Lepas Anatifera, and its corresponding species, by which they are attached to wood, &c.
Peduncle, a foot-stalk or tube on which anything is seated.
Pediform, foot-shaped.
Pelagic, belonging to the deep sea.
Pellicle, the skin or film.
Pellucid, transparent, clear, bright.
Pentagonal, having five angles.
Perforated, pierced with holes.
Pervious, admitting passage.
Phosphorescent, emitting light in the dark.
Pillar, in univalves is the internal continuation of the columella or inner lips, and extends from the *base* to the *apex*.
Pinnated, winged.
Plaited, folded.
Plaits, folds.
Plicated, folded or plaited, as in the pillar of the volute tribe.
Plumose, having a feathery appearance.
Polythalmous, divided into several chambers.
Porcate, marked with raised longitudinal lines.
'orrected, projecting.
Prismatic, generally applied to the colours of shells, being like those of the prism; iridescent.
Produced, lengthened out.
Protrude, to thrust forward.
Protuberances, plaits higher or more elevated than the parts adjoining.
Punctuated, with small hollows like the punctures of a thimble.
Pyriform, pear-shaped.

Q.

Quadrangular, having four right angles.
Quadriplicated, having four plaits.

R.

Radiated, furnished with rays.
Radicated, is when the shell is fixed by the base to another body.
Rectangular, having right angles.
Recurvated, turned backward.
Recurved, bowed back.

Reflected, thrown backward, or bent back.
Reflex, } the same as *recurvated*.
Reflexed, }
Refracted, abruptly bent, as if broken.
Reniform, kidney-shaped.
Repand, with a serpentine margin.
Replicated, folded or plaited, so as to form a groove or channel.
Reticulated, formed like a piece of network.
Retroflected, bent backward.
Retrousse, cocked up, turned up.
Retroverted, turned back.
Retuse, ending in an obtuse sinus.
Retundated, blunted, or turned at the edge.
Reversed spire, is when the volutions turn the reverse way of a common corkscrew, or to the sun's apparent motion.
Revolute, rolled backward.
Ribbed, having longitudinal or transverse ridges.
Ridge, the upper part of a slope.
Rima, the interstice between the valves when the hymen is removed.
Rostrum, the beak; the extension of the shell, in which the canal is situated.
Rotund, round, circular, spherical.
Rudimentary, the commencement or first elements of anything; generally applied to the indistinct teeth of shells.
Rufous, of a reddish colour.
Rugose, rugged, full of wrinkles.

S.

Sanguinaceous, of a blood colour, or resembling blood.
Scabrous, rough, rugged, harsh, or like a file.
Scalloped, indented at the edges.
Scorbiculate, pitted, having the surface covered with hollows.
Scorbiculous, a depression or cavity.
Scutellated, } shield-shaped.
Scutelliform, }
Seam, the line formed by the union of the valves.
Semi, is used in composition in the sense of half.
Semi-cordate, half heart-shaped.
Semi-cylindrical, half cylindrical, cut through lengthways.
Semi-orbicular, the shape of a half globe.
Semi-lunar, the shape of a half moon.

Semi-pellucid, somewhat pellucid or shining.
Septiform, in the shape of a partition.
Serrated, like the teeth of a saw.
Serrulated, very minutely serrated.
Sessile, sitting or seated.
Seta, a bristle.
Setaceous, bristly, covered with bristles.
Setiferous, bearing bristles.
Setose, covered with bristles.
Sinister valve, is the left valve.
Sinus, a groove or cavity.
Siphunculus, a cylindrical canal perforating the partitions in polythalmous shells; for instance, as in the *Nautilus Spirula*.
Solitary, generally applied to a single tooth in bivalves.
Spatulate, rounded and broad at the top, and becoming narrow like a spatula or battledore.
Species, the division of a family or genus, containing such as agree with it in general characters, or such as are derived from one common parentage.
Spiny, thorny, covered with thorn-like processes.
Spinous, having spines like a hedgehog.
Spire, all the whorls of univalve shells, excepting the one in which the aperture is situated, which is termed the *body*.
Spiral, twisted like a corkscrew.
Squamose, scaly.
Stellated, starred, consisting of star-like figures.
Striated, scored, or covered with fine threadlike lines.
Sub, in composition, means almost, or approaching to; as sub-globose, somewhat globular.
Sub-arcuated, somewhat arched.
Sub-conic, somewhat conical.
Sub-diaphanous, somewhat transparent or clear.
Sub-rotund, nearly globular.
Subulate, awl-shaped.
Sulcated, furrowed.
Sulci, furrows or ridges.
Summit, the tip or apex.
Sature, a hollow line of division in univalve shells, the spiral line of which separates the wreaths.

T.

Tentacula, the feelers of snails which inhabit shells.

Tesselated, checkered like a chess-board.
Testacea, the third order of worms, including those which are covered with a testaceous shell.
Testaceous, consisting of carbonate of lime and animal matter.
Tetragonal, four cornered.
Torose, swelling into knobs or protuberances.
Tortuosity, wreath, flexure.
Tortuous, twisted, wreathed, winding.
Transverse, placed across or crossways. When the breadth of a shell is greater than its length, it is called transverse.
Trapeziform, shaped like a trapezium.
Trigonal, having three angles.
Truncated, stunted, cut short or abruptly off at the end.
Tubercle, a little knot or pimple.
Tuberculated, knotted, pimpled.
Tuberosities, prominent knots or excrescences.
Tubular, in the shape of a hollow tube.
Tubulate, tubulous or hollow.
Tunicated, coated.
Turbinated, shaped like a top or pear.
Turgid, swollen.

U & V.

Valve, the whole of univalve shells, of shells in one piece; and the half of bivalves, or shells in two divisions, &c.
Varices, longitudinal ribs in univalve shells.
Variety, is when one species differs some little degree from that of another.
Vaulted, like the roof of one's mouth.
Venter, the belly, situated in the body of the shell; being the most prominent part when the aperture is turned to the observer.
Ventral, belonging to the belly.
Ventricose, inflated, swelled in the middle.
Vermiform, worm-shaped.
Vertex, in the Patella the top or most prominent part, situated in general nearly in the middle. In the genus Bulla it is used for the apex.
Verrucose, warted.
Verticulated, whorled.
Umbilicated, having a depression in the centre like a navel.
Umbo, in bivalve shells, the round part which turns over the hinge.

GLOSSARY.

Umbonate, bossed, having a raised knob in the centre
Undulated, waved, having a waved surface.
Ungulate, shaped like a horse's hoof.
Unilocular, with a single chamber or compartment.
Univalve, shells consisting of one valve or piece.
Volutions, the wreaths or turnings of the shells of univalves.
Urceolate, swelling in the middle like a pitcher.
Valva, a spatulated mark in several bivalve shells; formed when the valves are united on the posterior and anterior slopes.

W.

Whorl, one of the wreaths or turnings of the spire of univalves.

Z.

Zigzag, having contrary turnings and windings.
Zoned, surrounded with one or more girdles.

INDEX

TO THE

CLASSES, FAMILIES, GENERA, AND PLATES.

[N.B.—The Classes are printed in Small Capitals, the Families in Italics, and the Genera in the Ordinary Type.]

A.

Acasta *one of the Oceanides*	.	2	1	4		20
Acera	.	4	4	1		101
Achatina	.	4	7	8	18	1—3	113
Alata	.	4	17	3		149
Amphidesma	.	3	5	7	6	9	39
Amphitritea	.	1	3	4		13
Amphitrite	.	1	3	4		14
Ampullaria	.	4	10	3	21	3	120
Anastoma	.	4	7	3		109
Anatifera	.	2	1	7	4	5	21
Anatina	.	3	4	2	12	5	33
Ancillaria	.	4	20	4	30	5	169
Ancylus	.	4	3	7	32	3	101
ANNELIDES	.	1	4			11
Anodonta	.	3	13	3	11	2, 3	68
Anomia	.	3	19	5	16	1	89
Aplysiacea	.	4	5	2		103
Aplysia	.	4	5	1		103
Arca	.	3	11	2	10	5	63
Arenicola	.	1	1	1		11
Arcacea	.	3	11	4		61
Argonauta	.	4	22	1	35	1, 2	176
Aspergillum	.	3	1	1	33	3	23
Auricula	.	4	7	10	19	6	115
Avicula	.	3	17	4	14	3	79

B.

Balanus	.	2	1	3	4	1	19
Brachiopoda	.	3	20	3		89
Buccinum	.	4	18	9	20	1	159
Bulimus	.	4	7	7	19	7	112
Bulla	.	4	4	3	17	7	102
Bullacea	.	4	4	3		101
Bullæa	.	4	4	2	17	5	102

C.

Calyptracea	4	3	7			97
Calyptræa	4	3	5	32	4	100
Canalifera	4	16	11			138
Cancellaria	4	16	4	25	5	142
Capsa	3	8	9	8	7	49
Cardiacea	3	10	5			57
Cardita	3	10	2	10	3	59
Cardium	3	10	1	10	2	58
Carinaria	4	22	2			176
Carocolla	4	7	2	19	1	108
Cassidaria	4	10	1	27	5	152
Cassis	4	18	2	28	5	153
Castalia	3	12	2	11	5	65
Chama	3	14	1	12	2	69
Cerithium	4	16	1	24	3	139
Chamacea	3	14	3			69
Chiton	4	2	3	1	1—4	95
Chitonellus	4	2	2			93
Cineras	2	1	9			22
CIRRHIPEDES	2	1				17
Cirrhipedes	2	1	10			17
Clausilia	4	7	8	19	3	111
Clavagella	3	1	2	—		23
Cleodora	4	1	3			92
Clio	4	1	2			92
Clymene	1	2	1			12
Colimacea	4	7	11			105
Columbella	4	19	1	29	6	161
Columellaria	4	19	5			160
Conchacea	3	9	7			49
CONCHIFERA	3	20				23
Convoluta	4	20	6			166
Conus	4	20	6	31	1, 2	174
Corbis	3	8	6	8	1	46
Corbula	3	6	1	6	6	39
Corbulacea	3	6	2			39
Concholepas	4	18	6	28	1	156
Coronula	2	1	2	4	3	19
Crania	3	19	6	16	4	89
Crassatella	3	5	3	6	4	37
Crassina	3	8	10	6	1	49
Crenatula	3	17	1	14	2	76
Crepidula	4	3	6	32	2	101
Creusia	2	1	5	4	2	20
Cuculæa	3	11	1	10	1	61
Cyclas	3	9	1	9	7	50
Cyclostoma	4	7	11	19	5	116
Cymbulia	4	1	5			93
Cyrena	3	9	2	6	7	51
Cypræa	4	20	1	34	4	169
Cypricardia	3	10	3	10	6	60
Cyprina	3	9	4	9	2	52
Cytherea	3	9	5	9	4	54

D.

Delphanula	4	14	3	23	5	131
Dentalium	1	2	2	33	1	12
Dolabella	4	5	2			103
Dolium	4	18	8	29	4	157
Donax	3	8	8	8	4	48
Dorsaliæ	1	1	2			11

E.

Eburna	4	18	10	29	3	159
Emarginula	4	3	2	32	5	98
Erycina	3	5	4	6	5	37
Etheria	3	14	2	11	1	71

F.

Fasciolaria	4	16	5	25	4	142
Fissurella	4	3	3	32	1	99
Fistulana	3	1	3	33	5	24
Fusus	4	16	6	25	3	143

G.

Galathea	3	9	3	6	8	51
Galeolaria	1	4	4			16
Gastrochæna	3	2	2	3	1	28
Glycimeris	3	3	4			31
Gryphea	3	19	1	16	2	85

H.

Haliotis	4	12	4	22	4, 6	127
Harpa	4	18	7	29	2	156
Helicina	4	7	4	19	4	109
Helix	4	7	1	18	4—9	107
Heteropoda	4	22	2			175
Hiatella	3	10	4	10	4	60
Hippopus	3	15	2	12	1	72
Hyalea	4	1	1			92
Hyria	3	13	2	5	4	67

I.

Iridina	3	13	4			69
Isocardia	3	10	5	12	4	61

J.

Janthina	4	11	5	18	6	125

L.

Lima	3	18	2	15	3	80
Limacinea	4	6	5			104
Limacina	4	1	4			93
Limax	4	6	3			104
Lingula	3	20	3	17	2	91

L. continued.

Lithophagi	3	7	3			40
Lucina	3	8	7	8	8	47
Lutraria	3	5	1			33
Lymnæcea	4	8	3			116
Lymnæ	4	8	3	21	1	117

M.

Mactracea	3	5	7			33
Mactra	3	5	2	9	6	36
Macrostomides	4	12	4			125
Magilus	1	4	5			16
Mallacea	3	17	5			76
Malleus	3	17	3	14	4	78
Maldania	1	2	2			12
Marginella	4	19	4	30	3	165
Melanides	4	9	3			117
Melania	4	9	1	20	3	118
Melanopsis	4	9	2	20	6	118
Meleagrina	3	17	5			79
Mitra	4	19	2	31	7	162
Modiola	3	16	2	12	6	74
MOLLUSCA	4	22				92
Monoceros	4	18	5			155
Monodonto	4	15	3	23	2	135
Murex	4	16	10	26	1, 3, 4	147
Myaria	3	4	2			32
Mya	3	4	1	5	1, 3	32
Mytilus	3	16	1			73
Mytilacea	3	16	3			78

N.

Naiades	3	13	4			66
Natica	4	11	4	21	6	124
Nautilacea	4	21	2			174
Nautilus	4	21	2	36	1, 3	175
Navicella	4	11	2			122
Nerita	4	11	3	21	5	123
Neritina	4	11	1	21	2, 4	121
Neritacea	4	11	5			121
Nucula	3	11	4	11	7	64
Nymphacea	3	8	10			42

O.

Oliva	4	20	5	30	1, 4	171
Onchidium	4	6	1			104
Orbicula	3	20	1	17	4	90
Ostrea	3	19	2	16	5	87
Ostracea	3	19	6			85
Otion	2	1	10			22
Ovula	4	20	1	34	1—4	166

P.

Paludina						
Parmacella	4	6	2			104
Parmophora	4	3	1			97
Patella	4	2	4	2	1—7	95
Pandora	3	6	2	6	3	40
Panopea	3	3	2	5	2	31
Pecten	3	18	3	15	4	82
Pectenaria	1	3	1			13
Pectunculus	3	11	3	11	6	64
Pedum	3	18	1	15	5	80
Pectinides	3	18	7			80
Peristomides	4	10	3			119
Perna	3	17	2	14	1	77
Petricola	3	7	2	7	3	41
Phasianella	4	15	6	24	2	137
Pholas	3	2	1	3	2—5	27
Pholadaria	3	2	2			26
Physa	4	8	2	20	2	117
Phyllidia	4	2	1			93
Phyllidiacea	4	2	4			93
Pirena	4	9	3			119
Pinna	3	16	3	13	1, 2	75
Pileopsis	4	3	4			99
Planorbis	4	8	1	20	4	116
Plicacea	4	13	2			128
Planaxis	4	15	5	27	4	136
Placuna	3	19	4	16	3	88
Pleurotoma	4	16	2	24	1	140
Plicatula	3	18	5	15	2	83
Plagiostoma	3	18	4			83
Pneumodermon	4	1	6			93
Pollicipes	2	1	8	4	4, 6	22
Podopsis	3	18	7			85
Psammobia	3	8	2	7	1	43
Psammotea	3	8	3	7	5	43
Pteroceras	4	17	2	28	3	150
Pteropoda	4	1	6			92
Pupa	4	7	5	18	5	110
Pupa	4	7	15	19	2	111
Purpura	4	18	4	28	4	155
Purpurifera	4	18	1			151
Pyramidella	4	13	2	22	5	129
Pyrula	4	16	7	25	6	144
Pyrgoma	2	1	6			21

R.

Ranella	4	16	2	25	2	145
Ricinula	4	18	3	26	2	153
Rostellaria	4	17	1	27	2	149

INDEX.

S.

Sabellaria	1	3	2	33	2	13
Sanguinolaria	3	8	1	7	4	42
Saxacavi	3	7	1	7	6	40
Scalaria	4	14	4	23	1	130
Scalarides	4	14	3			129
Septaria	3	1	4			25
Serpula	1	4	2			14
Serpulacea	1	4	5			14
Sigaretus	4	12	1	22	2	126
Siliquaria	1	1	2	33	4	11
Solarium	4	15	1	23	4	131
Solecurtus	3	3	3	31	6	31
Solen	3	3	1	31	5	29
Solenides	3	3	4			29
Solenimya	3	5	6	6	2	38
Spirorbis	1	4	1			14
Spirula	4	21	1	36	2	175
Spondylus	3	18	6	15	1	84
Stomatella	4	12	2	22	1	151
Stomatia	4	12	3	22	6	144
Strombus	4	17	3	28	2	126
Struthiolaria	4	16	9	25	1	198
Succinea	4	7	9	24	4	114

T.

Tellina	3	8	4	8	5	45
Tellinides	3	8	5	8	3	46
Terebella	1	3	3			14
Terebellum	4	20	3	31	3	169
Terebra	4	18	11	27	1, 3	160
Terebratula	3	20	2	17	1	90
Teredo	3	1	6			25
Teredina	3	1	5			25
Testacella	4	6	4	17	6	104
Tornatella	4	13	1	22	3	128
Trochus	4	15	2	23	6	133
Tridacna	3	15	1	12	2	71
Tridacnites	3	15	2			71
Trigonia	3	12	1	11	4	65
Trigonacea	3	12	2			65
Triton	4	16	11	26	5	148
Tubicola	3	1	6			23
Turbicinella	2	1	1			18
Turbo	4	15	4	24	6	136
Turbinacea	4	15	7			131
Turbinella	4	16	3			140
Turritella	4	15	7	24	3	139

U. V.

Ungulina	3	5	5			37
Unio	3	13	1	8	6	67
Valvata	4	10	1	20	5	119
Venericardia	3	9	7	9	1	57
Venerirupis	3	7	3	7	2	42
Venus	3	9	6	8	2, 3	56
Vermilia	1	4	3			15
Vermetus	4	14	1	23	3	129
Vitrina	4	6	5	17	3	104
Voluta	4	19	3	30	2	164
Volvaria	4	19	5	29	5	165
Vulsella	3	19	3	15	6	87

Pl. 1.

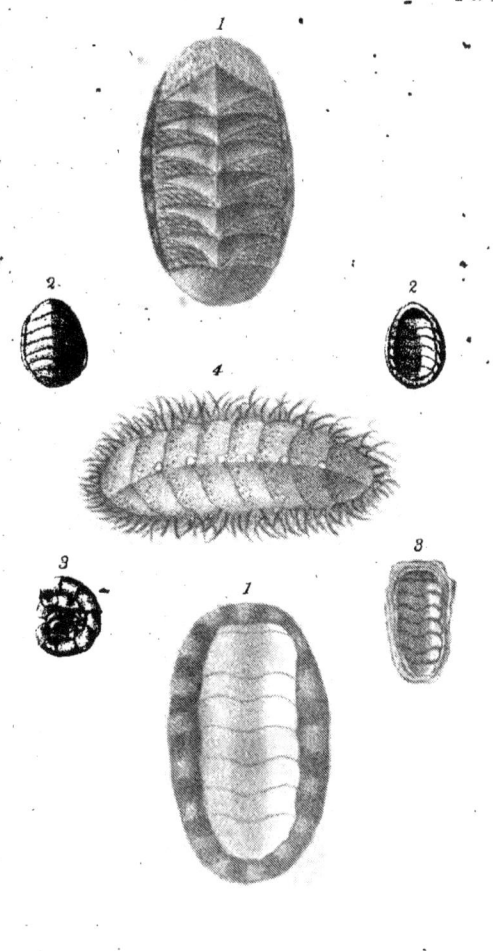

Pl. 2.

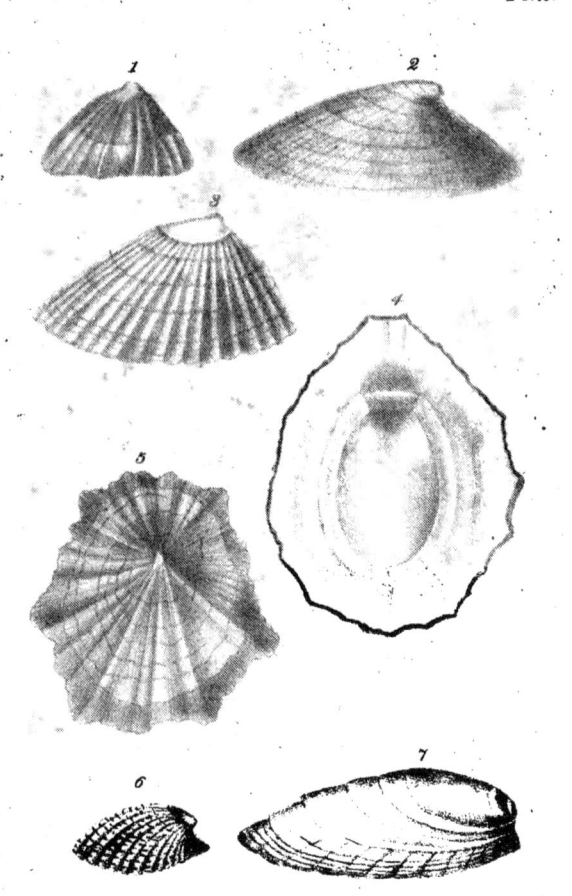

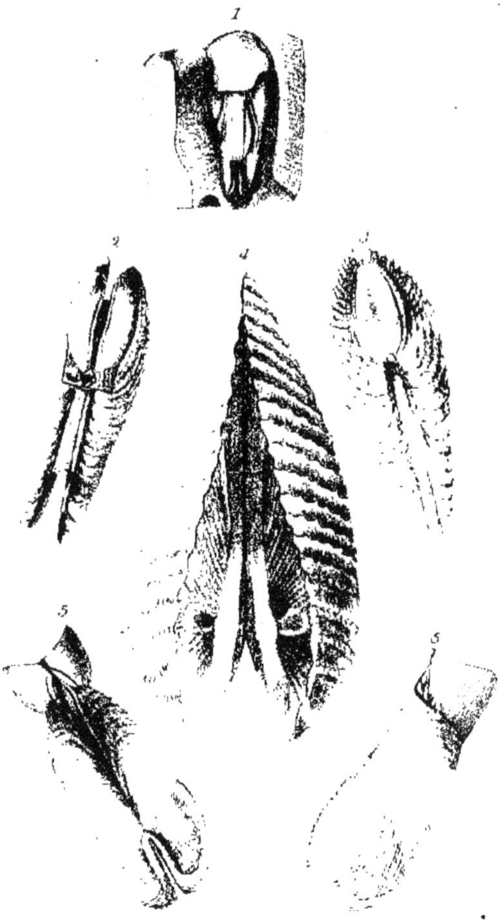

Lith. of D.W. Kellogg & Co Hartford Ct

Pl 4.

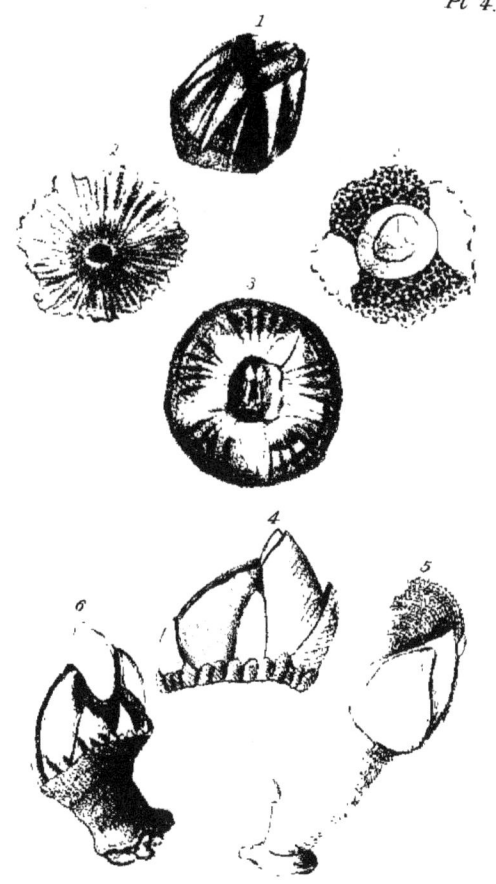

Lith. of D. W. Kellogg & Co. Hartford Ct.

Pl. 5

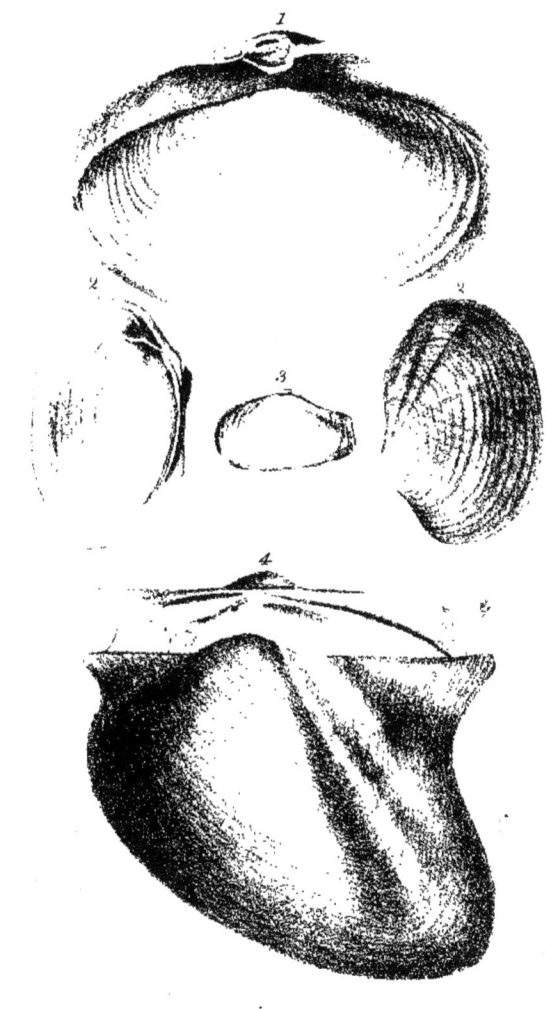

Lith. of D.W.Kellogg & Co. Hartford.

Pl. 6.

Pl. 7.

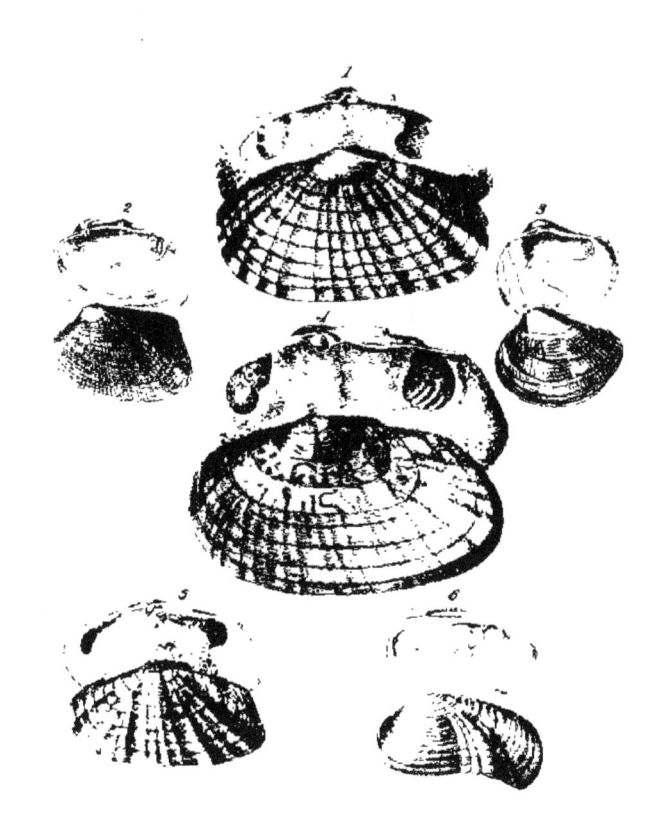

Pl. 8.

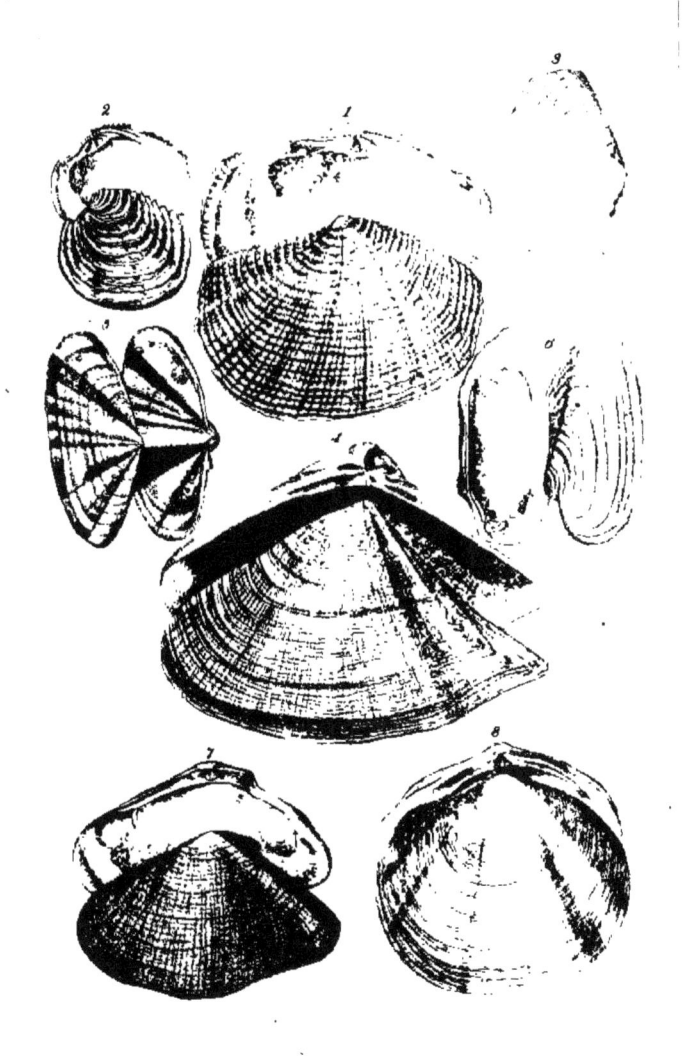

Pl. 9.

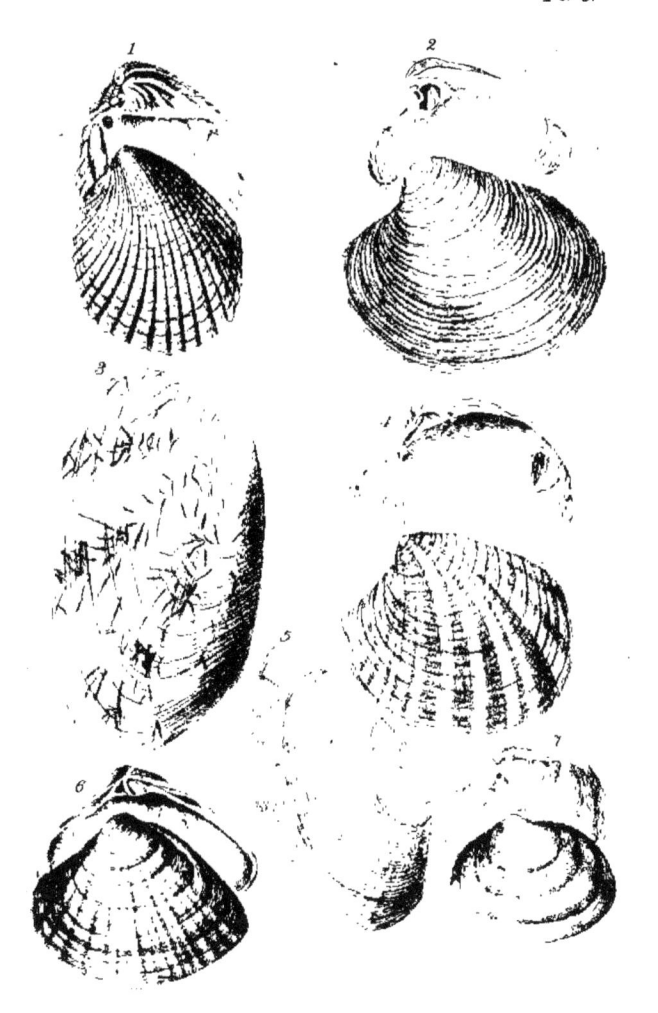

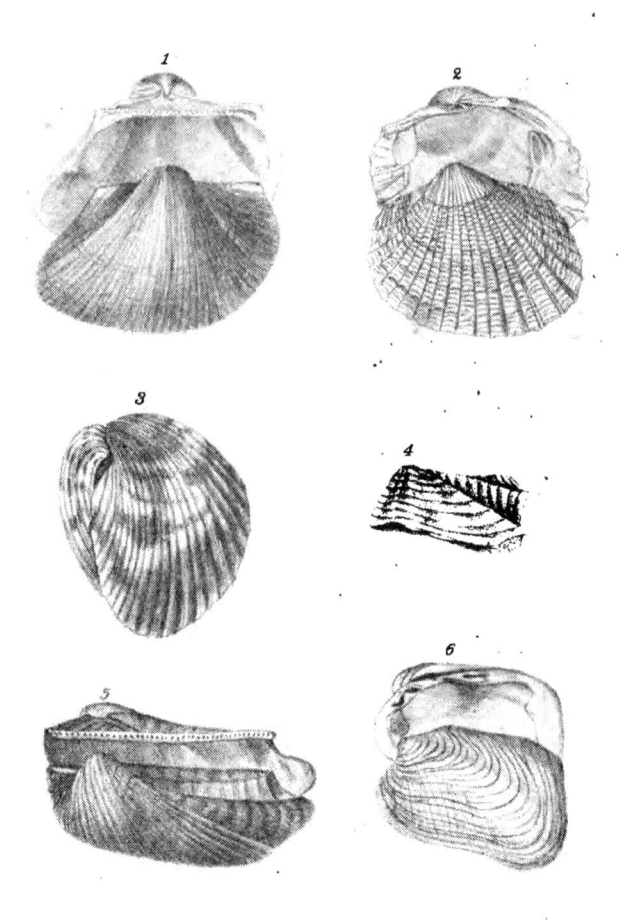

Lith. of D.W.Kellogg & Co. Hartford. Ct.

Pl. 11.

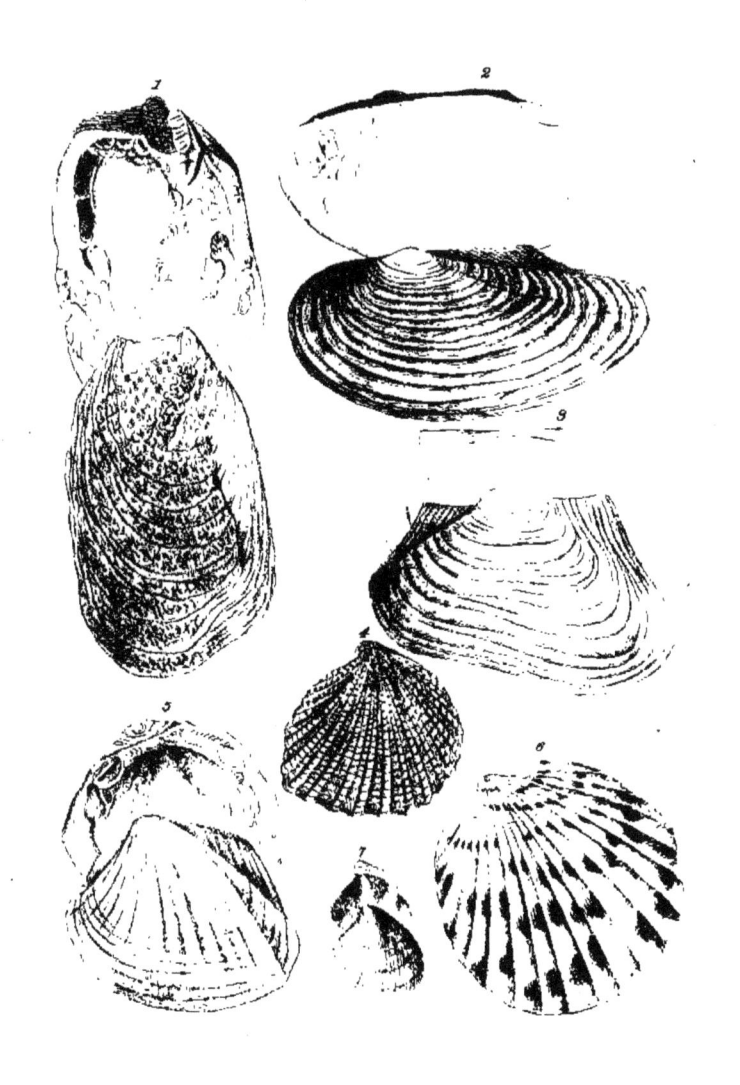

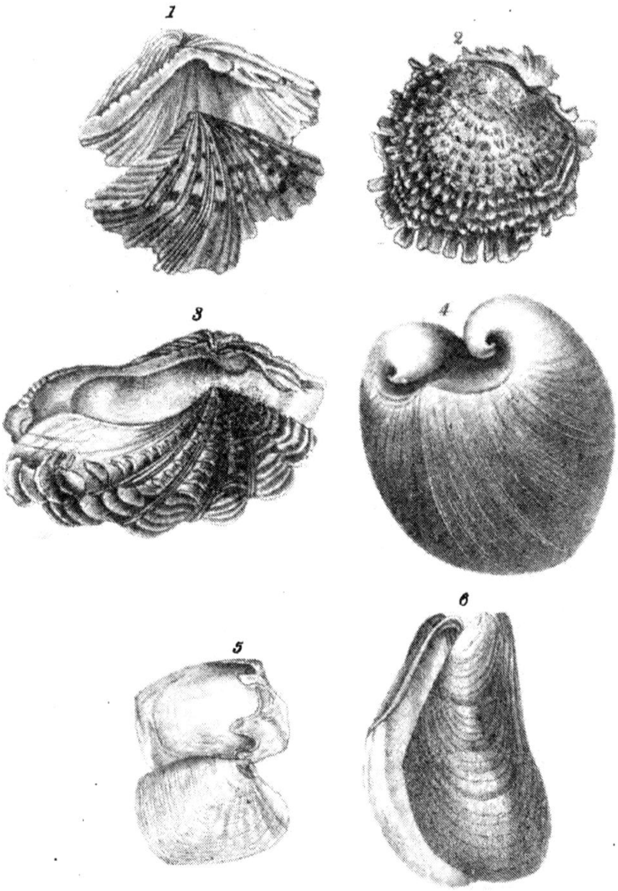

Lith. of D. W. Kellogg & Co. Hartford, Ct

Pl. 13

Pl. 14

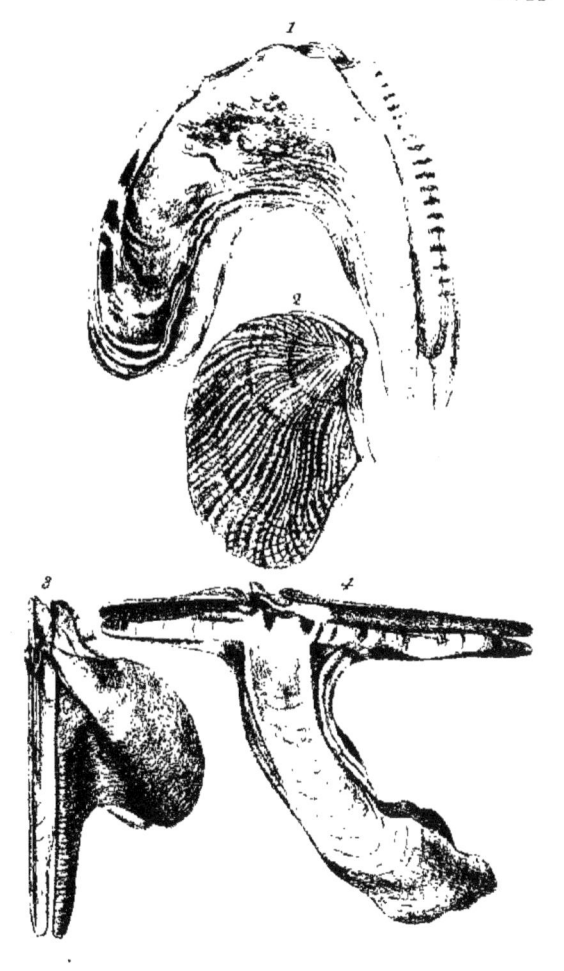

Lith. of D.W.Kellogg & Co. Hartford Ct.

Pl. 15.

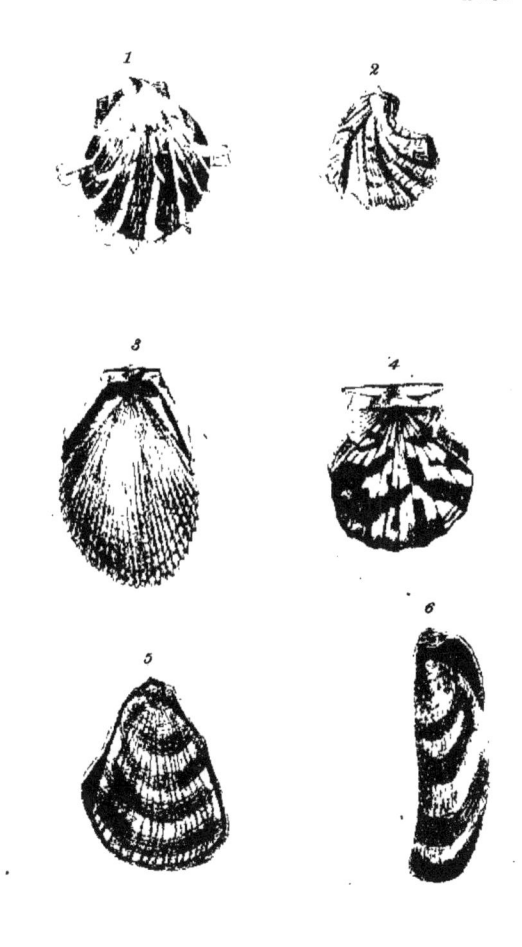

Lith. of D.W.Kellogg & Co Hartford. Ct.

Pl 16.

Lith. of D.W.Kellogg & Co. Hartford Ct.

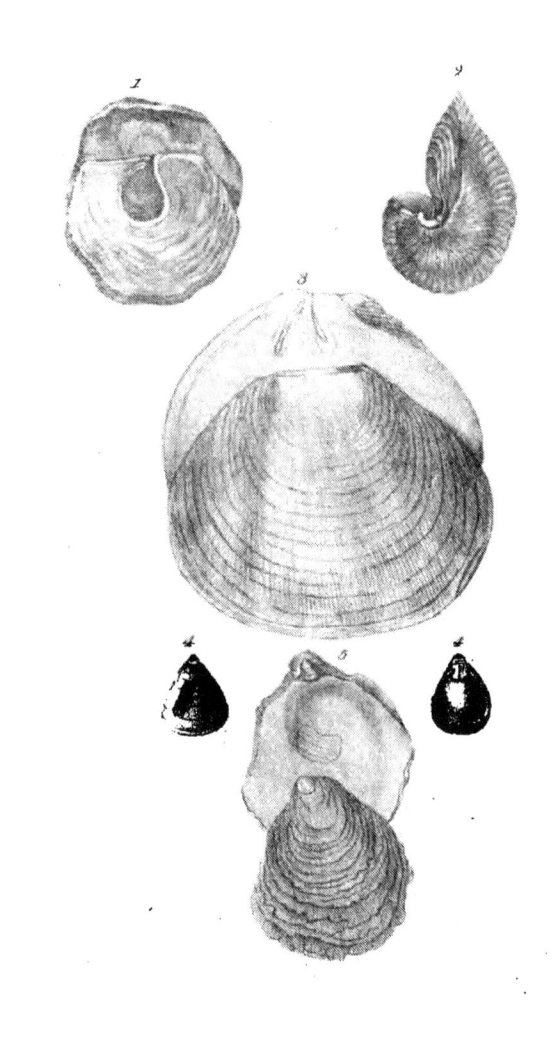

Pl. 17.

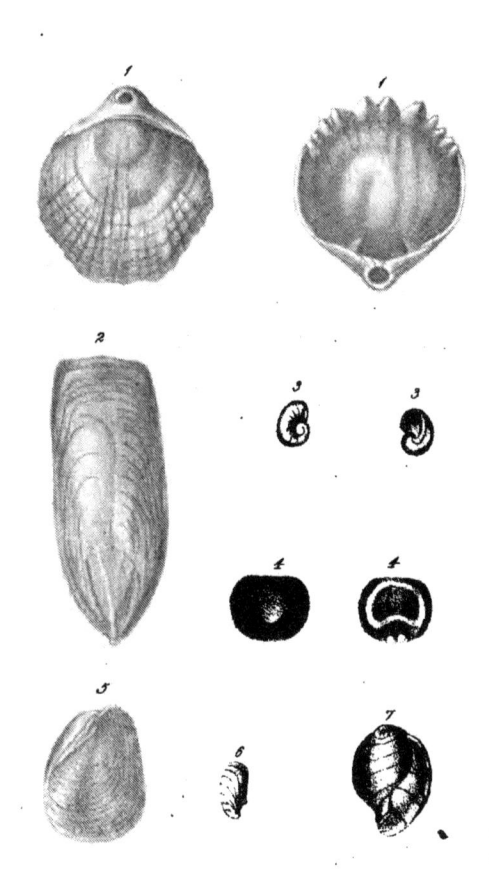

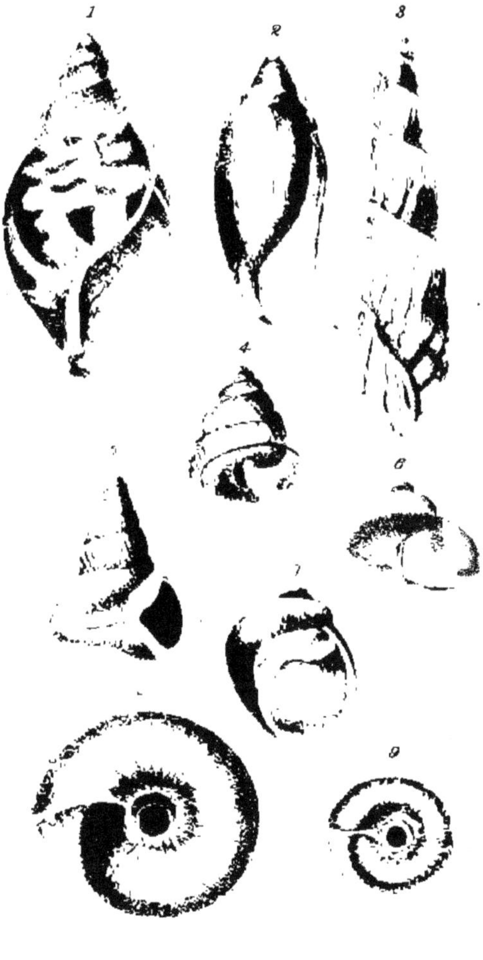
1
2
3
4
6
7
9

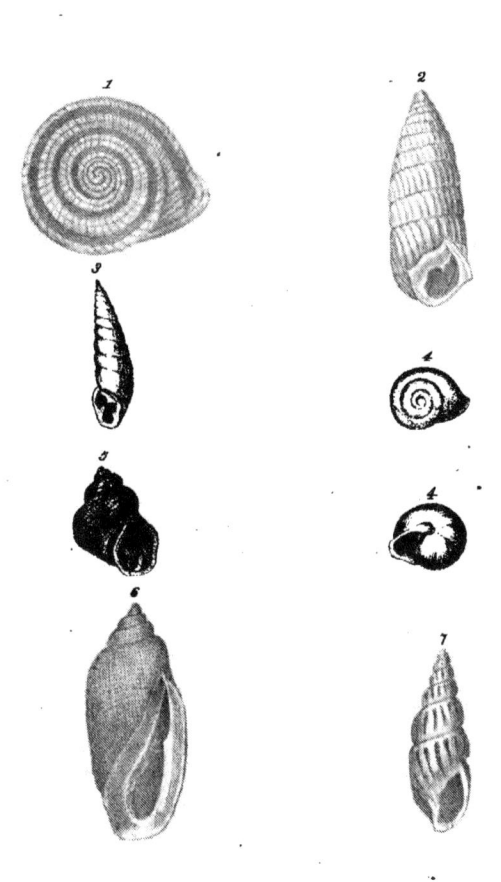

Lith. of D.W.Kellogg & Co. Hartford. Ct.

Pl. 20.

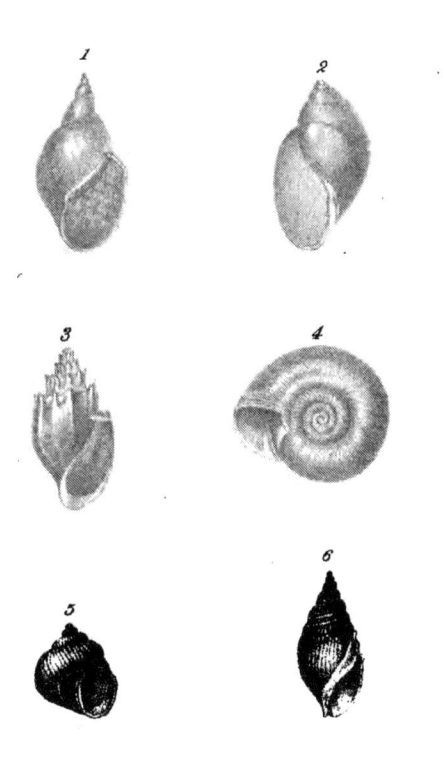

Pl. 21.

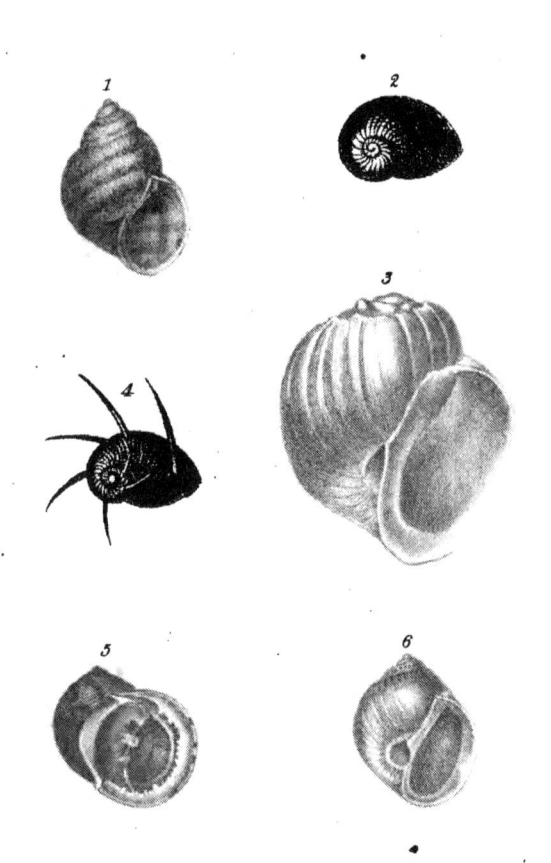

Lith. of D.W.Kellogg & Co. Hartford Ct.

Pl. 22.

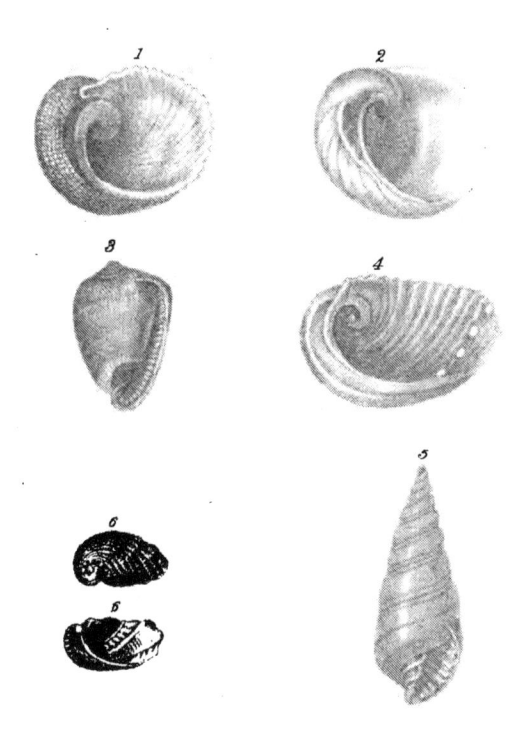

Pl. 23.

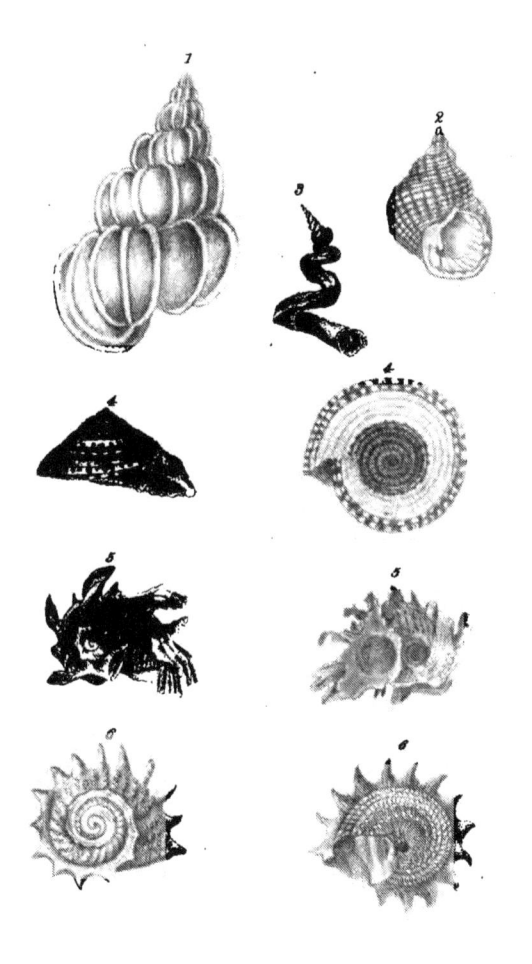

Pl. 24.

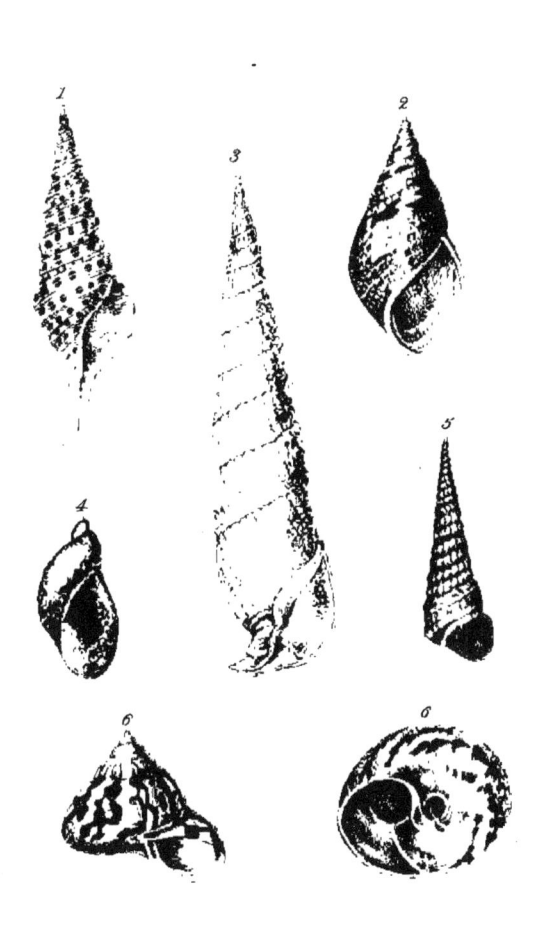

Pl. 25.

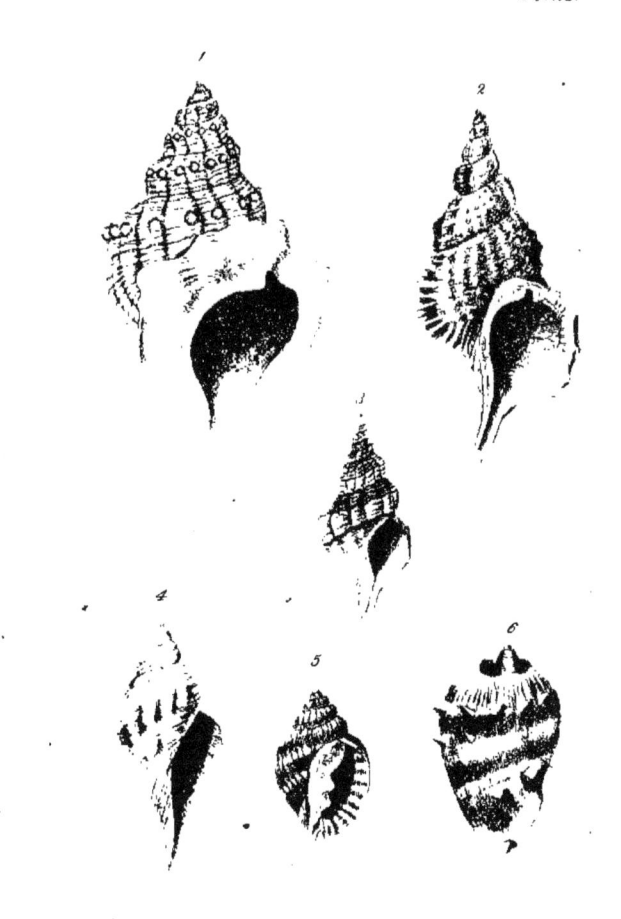

Lith. of D.W.Kellogg & Co. Hartford, Ct.

Pl. 26.

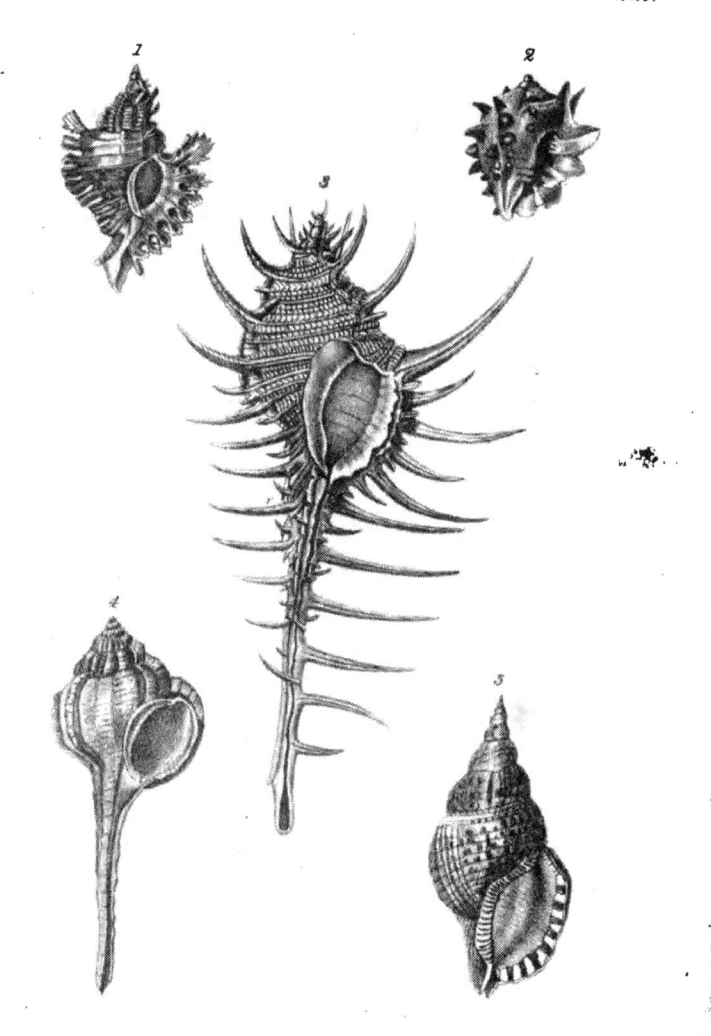

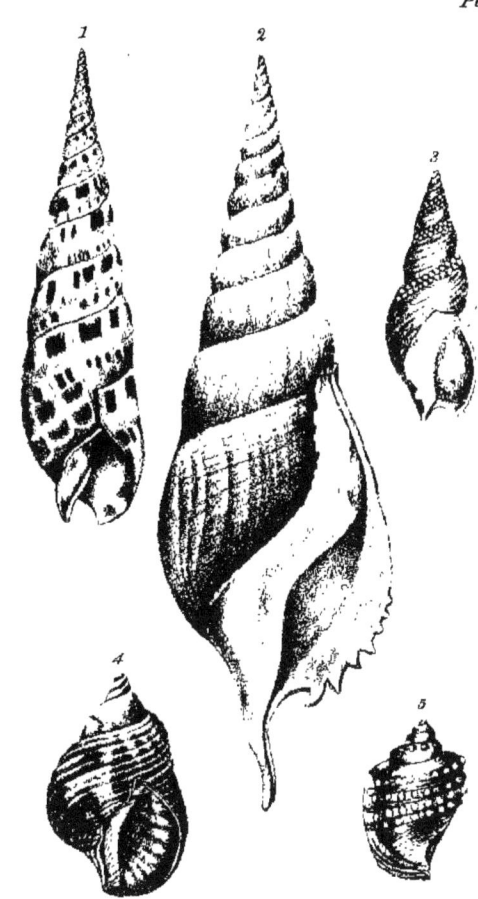

Pl

Lith of D.W.Kellogg & Co. Hartford. Co

Pl. 28

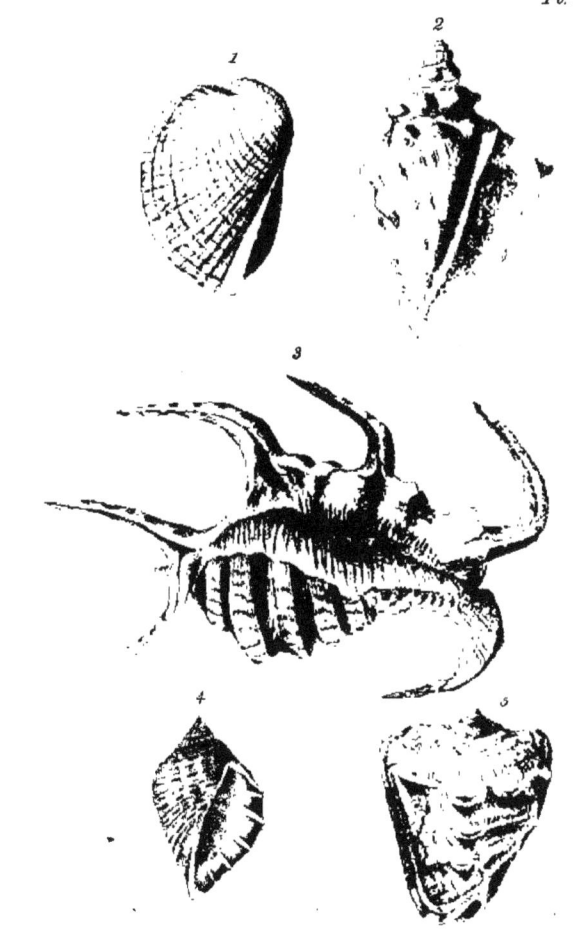

Lith. of D.W.Kellogg & Co. Hartford Ct

Lith. of D.W.Kellogg & Co. Hartford, Ct.

Lith of D.W.Kellogg & Co.

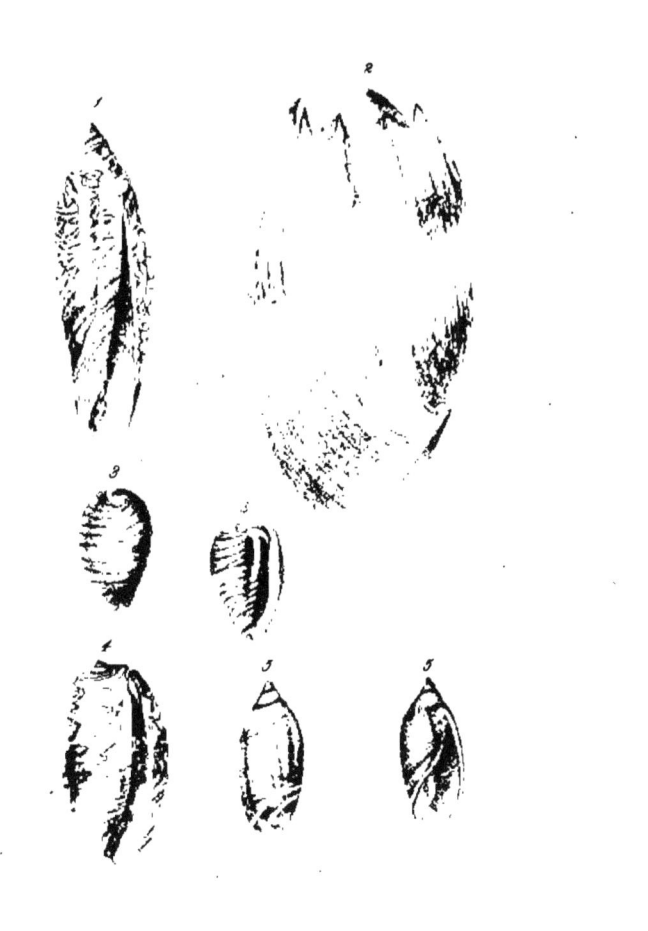

Pl. 31.

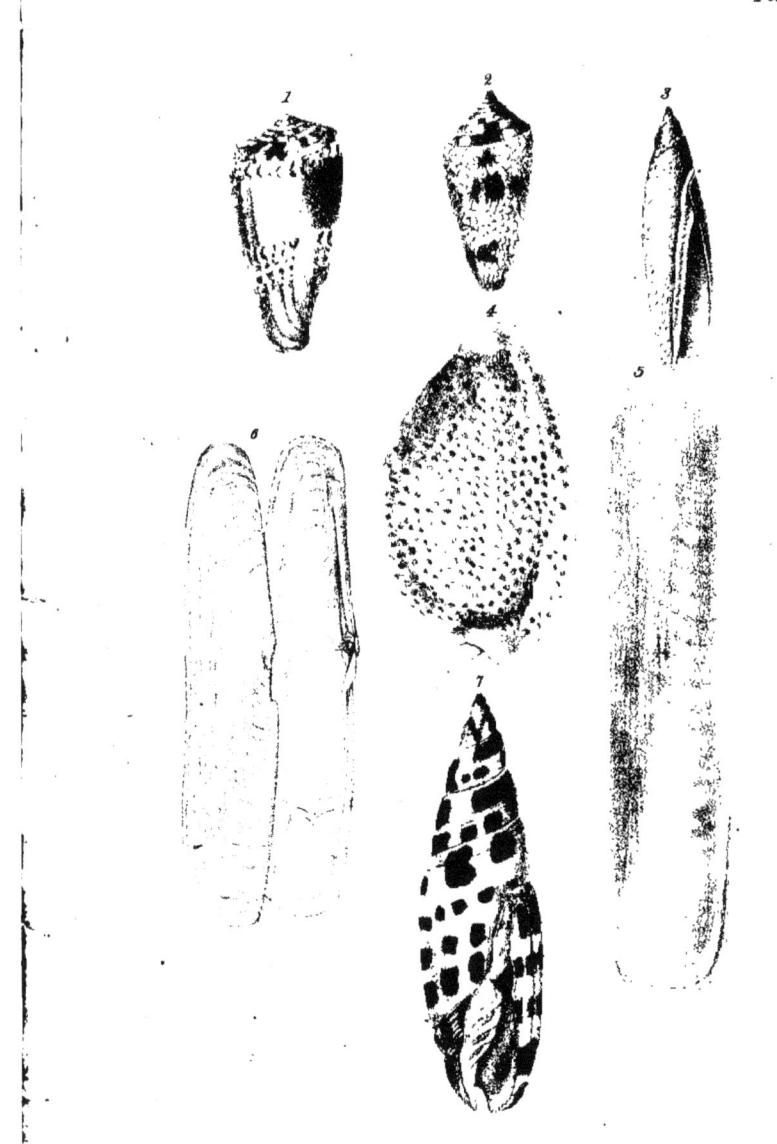

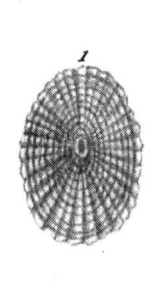

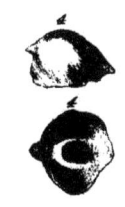

Lith. of D.W. Kellogg & Co. Hartford. Ct.

Pl. 33.

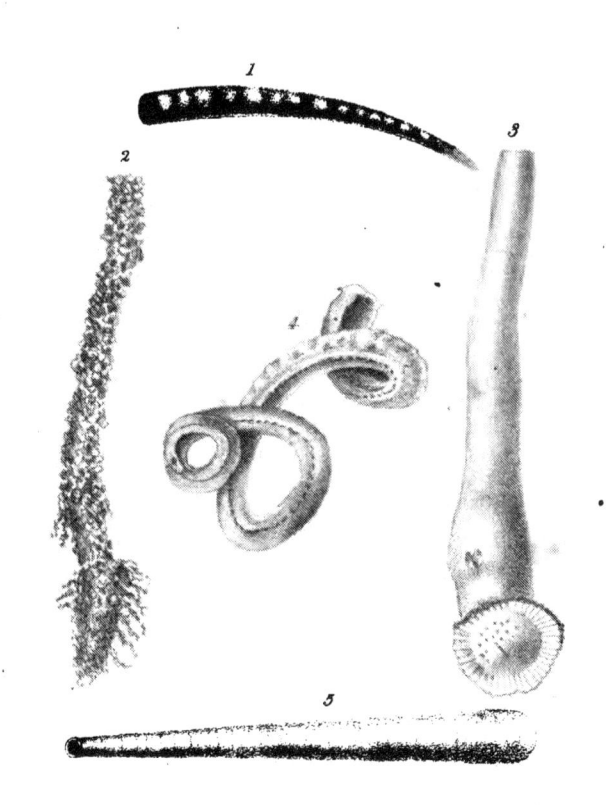

Lith. of D.W.Kellogg & Co. Hartford Ct.

1/pg 12 — 2/pg 13 — 3/pg 23 — 4/pg 11 — 5/pg 24

Pl. 84.

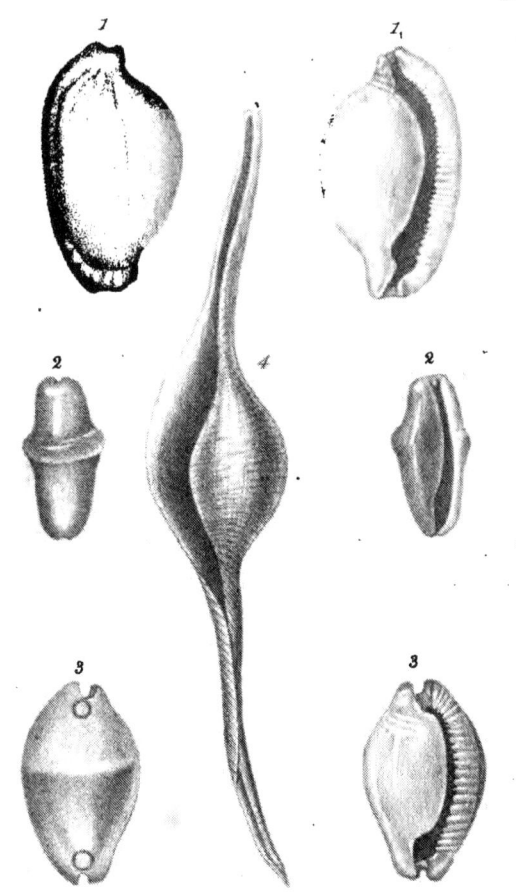

Pl. 35.

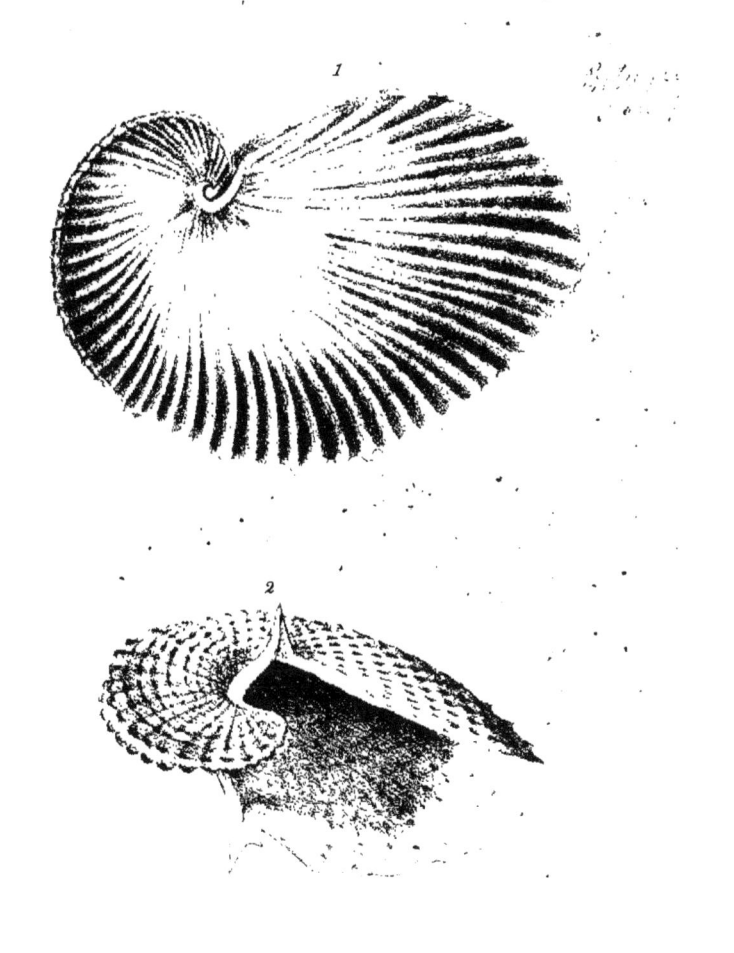

Pl. 36.

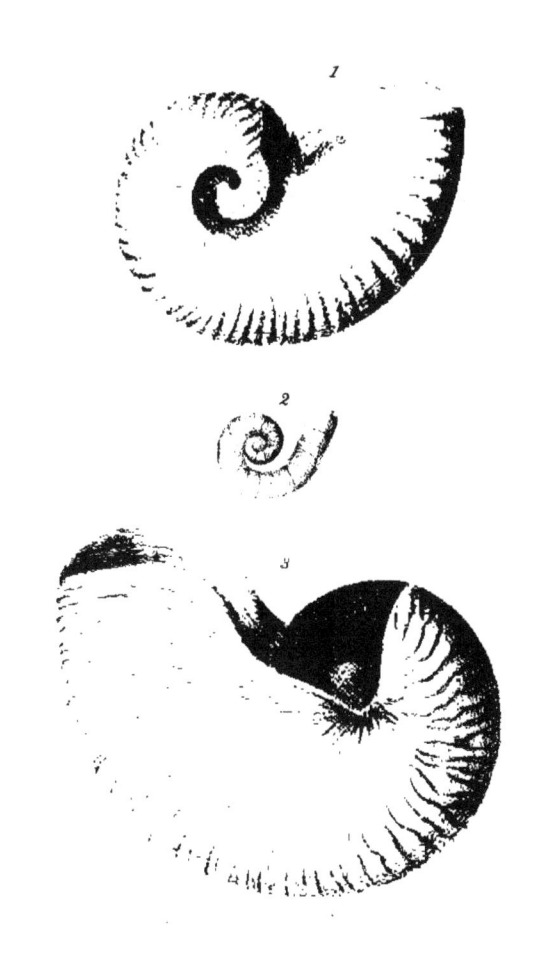

Printed in the USA
CPSIA information can be obtained
at www.ICGtesting.com
LVHW020226280524
781577LV00018B/201

9 781022 790131

CONCHOLOGY.   139

C nodulosum.	C. obtusum.
C. vulgatum.	C. semigranosum.
C. obeliscus.	C. asperum.
C. granulatum.	C. lineatum.
C. aluco.	C. vertagus.
C. echinatum.	C. fasciatum.
C. subulatum.	C. ocellatum.
C. heteroclites.	C. literatum.
C. zonale.	C. atratum.
C. semiferrugineum.	C. eburneum.
C. torulosum.	C. punctatum.
C. tuberculatum.	C. lima.
C. morus.	C. perversum.

C. vertagus. The curved beak Cerithium. Pl. 24, fig. 3.
Species with evidently a small canal, very short, and recurved obliquely towards the back.

C. aluco. The caterpillar Cerithium.
Species with a canal much smaller, but entirely straight, and a sinus well formed at the posterior union of the two edges.

C. semigranosum. The semigranulated Cerithium.
Fusiform, turreted; apex acute; the suture with double spiral rows of large granules; minutely striated transversely, with sulcated granulations; colour reddish brown.

2. Pleurotoma. Twenty-three species.

Distinguished from the Cerithium by having a notch or slit in the right margin.

Shell fusiform, rather rugged, spire turreted; aperture ovate, small, terminated by a canal variable in length; the right edge sharp, more or less notched; operculum horny.

Pleurotoma imperialis.	Pleurotoma fascialis.
P. auriculifera.	P. bimarginata.
P. muricata.	P. buccinoides.
P. echinata.	P. cingulifera.

P. flavidula.	P. virgo.
P. interrupta.	P. Babylonia.
P. crenularis.	P. undosa.
P. cincta.	P. marmorata.
P. unizonalis.	P. tigrina.
P. lineata.	P. crispa.
P. spirata.	P. albina.
P. nodifera.	

P. Babylonia. The Tower of Babel Pleurotoma. Pl. 24, fig. 1.

Species in which the tube is rather long, and the notch is a little posterior to the middle of the edge.

P. auriculifera. The eared Pleurotoma.

Species in which the tube is short, and the notch entirely against the spire.

P. nodifera. The knotty or Javanese Pleurotoma.

Species with outer lip largely notched and deeply crenulated; upper volution smooth; under volution and body striated transversely, with angulated oblique nodules at the suture; colour reddish yellow.

3. Turbinella. Twenty-three species.

By Linnæus this genus was classed with the Voluta, though they are more closely allied to the Murex; differing, however, from them by having no varices.

Shell generally turbinated, but sometimes turreted, rugged, and thick; spire variable in form; aperture elongated, terminated by a straight canal, often rather short; the left edge almost straight, and formed by a callosity which hides the columella; the right edge entire and sharp; the columella with two or three unequal, almost transverse plaits.

Turbinella scolymus.	Turbinella leucozonalis.
T. rapa.	T. rustica.
T. napus.	T. cingulifera.
T. pyrum.	T. polygonia.
T. pugillaris	T. carinifera.